Praise for *The Linked*

The LinkedIn Playbook is more than a LinkedIn guide on how to navigate the platform. Rather, it is an in-depth, behind the curtain reveal of best practices to turn this platform into an indispensable part of the savvy business owner's digital toolkit. I have applied some of Adam's strategies with great success and benefited directly from them. Thanks, Adam.

—Brad Beer, founder of POGO Physio, bestselling author, host of *The Physical Performance Show* podcast

Even an advanced LinkedIn user will get value from this book, which is full of the latest tactics to improve your social-selling practices.

—Alex Allwood, CEO of The Holla Agency, author of *Customer Experience is the Brand*

After getting such great value from Adam's first book, *Social Media Secret Sauce*, I was expecting a tonne of value from *The LinkedIn Playbook*. And a tonne of value is exactly what Adam delivers. This book provides practical advice and easy-to-follow steps on getting the most out of LinkedIn. Straightaway I could see what I was doing wrong and the simple tweaks I could implement immediately to optimise my profile for greater impact. Thanks to Adam and *The LinkedIn Playbook*, I have a far greater understanding of how to use LinkedIn effectively, and how to use the platform to better serve and connect with my industry.

—Katie Marshall, founder of Chicks and Mortar, author of *Chicks and Mortar*

Difficult to put down, jam-packed with practical solutions, this book is a must-read for anyone wanting to build their LinkedIn profile to all-star status (top five percent). [Adam Houlahan's] tips and tricks ensure that your targeted audience will naturally gravitate to you because you are demonstrating that you're a person of influence in your industry.

—Jules Blundell, director of VideoBuzz, author of *Capture More Customers with Video*, regular contributor to Smallville and MOB

Adam Houlahan really knows this stuff. If you're after the strategies to create a large following of trusted, loyal and buying fans, then follow Adam on his quest to reveal the inner workings of social-media psychology. *The LinkedIn Playbook* is no exception, and is an easy-to-follow guide on creating true connections with your wanted target market.

—Grant Kennedy, We Shoot Buildings, author of *Beyond the Build*

As a prolific user of LinkedIn, I've purchased several books and courses on using LinkedIn to date. We also advise all our clients on how to use LinkedIn and help them with strategy and content. Adam's *The LinkedIn Playbook* is the best resource we've come across when it comes to giving the right balance of why, what and how. I love the way he shares his own stories and those of his clients so you can see the advice in action.

I also appreciate his advice on things not to do. He doesn't hold anything back, which provides proof of his own adherence to the wonderful concept of giving, and is the reason behind his own pre-eminence in the world of social media. I highly recommend this book to anyone wanting to know what to do on LinkedIn, and how to do it properly.

I think this will be a great gift for some of my clients. It's one of those books that, as you read it, you need to have LinkedIn open and start putting all the great advice into action immediately.

—Annette Welsford, CEO of Commonsense Marketing, Brisbane (commonsensemarketing.com.au)

My ideal audience can be found on LinkedIn, a forum I was introduced to just after it was founded about eleven years ago. I have been studying and learning about this potential medium for many years, but no one has broken it down as simply or effectively as Adam Houlahan has in this book. He sets out the best step-by-step process to enhance your success on LinkedIn. If you are serious about becoming a lot more successful in getting to the right people on LinkedIn, read this book. I know my success on LinkedIn will be improved thanks to the valuable information in *The LinkedIn Playbook*.

—Daryl La'Brooy, founder and CEO of Business Ownership Protection Specialists, author of *Business Ownership Bullet-Proofed*

For most business owners, LinkedIn promises the world but in practice just becomes a huge drain on time and resources. In this excellent follow-up to his highly successful first book, *Social Media Secret Sauce*, Adam provides a practical, easy-to-follow guide for effectively converting LinkedIn contacts to customers. His clear guidance, insightful tips and straightforward methods will quickly put LinkedIn at the heart of your sales and marketing strategies.

—Geoff Green, business exit strategist, founder of GRG Momentum, author of *The Smart Business Exit*

Having been a LinkedIn user since early 2004 (yes, my user ID number is in the 165-thousand range), having currently 25000+ followers, 3000+ connections, an overall SSI index score of 81 out of 100, an industry SSI of 1 percent and a network SSI of 2 percent, I considered myself a LinkedIn pro. Even so, Adam's book offered some key insights that I did not know how and/or why to apply. Reading it prompted me to review my tagging strategy as well as update the 'prime real estate' section, which is what shows up first when people search for me. I expect that it will increase the number of inbound opportunities and my conversion. Lesson learnt? That even if you think you are proficient, there is always something that can be done better or which needs tweaking. The job is just never done.

—Carsten Primdal, CEO of Vantage Compliance & Mitigation, author of *Red Flag*

If you want to be in charge of your LinkedIn relationship building and prospect marketing, then I recommend you start with this great book. Adam Houlahan takes you by the hand and leads you through a learning journey to become a player rather than a bystander.

—Per Lillie, MD of Pro Business Coaching, author of *Remove Blocks & Build Your Business*

If LinkedIn is where your potential customers or clients are, then *The LinkedIn Playbook* is essential reading. The author takes the reader logically through the steps to set up a profile, link with others and then engage with them. It's easy to read and very practical, with examples that you can use as is or adjust to suit your personality and business brand.

—Amanda Fisher, The Numbers Matter,
author of *Unscramble Your Numbers*

Adam's book delivers actionable advice through a complete all-in-one-guide. With clever and practical strategies, *The LinkedIn Playbook* will leave you and your marketing team with an easy-to-implement roadmap. I am using it with my team at a NFP; it's brilliant.

—Anoushka Gungadin, bestselling author of The Nurtured Woman series, CEO, The Duke of Edinburgh's International Award, Australia

Adam's book is a must-read for anyone who has been or is confused by LinkedIn. It's a step-by-step guide to building an excellent profile and a professional network. *The LinkedIn Playbook* also provides instructions on how to leverage your profile and your network to reach business or personal goals.

—Beth Powell, founder of Digital Marketing
Club, author of *Drive More Business*

LinkedIn has great potential for every entrepreneur and business owner, but using it well requires a good deal of knowledge and skill. *The LinkedIn Playbook* teaches you how, offering a step-by-step practical guide to make LinkedIn really work. What's more, Adam has based his guidance on social serving rather than social selling, which (for me) is a triple win—that's wins for you, for those you work with, and the world. This book will live on my desk as an invaluable reference.

—Rosemary Shapiro-Liu, director of Triple Win Enterprises, author of *The Mentor Within*

The LinkedIn Playbook gives you the information, ideas and insights to really connect with LinkedIn and your audience on this platform. Gone are the days of having thousands of people as part of your network. Now you have the ability to leverage these conversations and connections for real business traction. Oftentimes we are mislead about the why and the how; Adam Houlahan gives you the clarity and real reasons for what you need to make happen on LinkedIn. It is a very thorough and helpful book for mastering the art of LinkedIn for beginners and experts alike.

—Doyle Buehler, global CEO of The Department of Digital, author of *The Digital Delusion*

Adam Houlahan is truly a social-media expert. He not only provides excellent and easy-to-follow instructions on how to increase your LinkedIn profile, but also explains the holistic view that surrounds social media, a view that many people do not realise. If you want to improve your LinkedIn profile, this book is a must-read for you.

—Sandra D'Souza, author of *Social Media for Baby Boomers*

The

LinkedIn

PLAY

BOOK

ADAM HOULAHAN

Published by Stenica Pty Ltd 2016

Copyright © 2016 Adam Houlahan

First Edition 2016

A catalogue record for this book is available from the National Library of Australia.

Book cover design and formatting services by BookCoverCafe.com

www.AdamHoulahan.com

978-0-9924698-3-2 (pbk)
978-0-9924698-2-5 (e-bk)

Contents

Foreword   xiii

Introduction   xvii

PART I   **1**

Chapter 1   START WITH WHY   3

Why do you want to use social media?   6

Why do you think LinkedIn is the best platform for you?   7

What is your company's why?   8

Elite500   9

Tayabali Tomlin   10

Ceebeks Business Solutions   12

Chapter 2   SEVEN ROOKIE MISTAKES YOU MUST AVOID   14

Content *not* to post   15

Privacy settings   16

Adding your connections to your email database   16

Over-posting updates and Pulse articles   17

Spamming your groups   18

Self-promotion   19

Not personalising messages   20

Chapter 3   SOCIAL SERVING VERSUS SOCIAL SELLING   22

What is social selling?   22

What is social serving?   25

Chapter 4   CREATING PRE-EMINENCE   27

How to become pre-eminent   30

Instil trust in your superior knowledge   32

The long-term value of networking   35

Chapter 5   YOU GET WHAT YOU GIVE   38

Creating impact   40

Examples of excellence   42

Charitable giving   45

Buy one give one   48

Chapter 6   QUICK RECAP   51

It's all in the profile   53

Your LinkedIn profile is not your resume   55

Keyword optimisation   56

Pictures speak a thousand words   59

Optimising your profile   62

Professional headline   63

Chapter 7   PREPARE FOR SUCCESS   83

Critical drivers and key-performance indicators   84

Keeping records   87

Scripts   88

Chapter 8   GETTING STARTED   98

Your client avatar   98

The law of reciprocity   100

Daily tasks   102

Profile viewing   103

Check your messages   105

Accept connection requests   107

Connecting with potential clients   107

Congratulations message   108

Welcome messages   108

Updating your spreadsheets   109

Free-gift messages   110

Third message   110

Chapter 9   OUTSOURCING   **112**

Finding virtual assistants   113

Account security   114

Chapter 10 MOVING THE CONVERSATION OFFLINE   **117**

How and when to ask for the call   119

Skype versus phone   124

Seven steps to a pre-eminent sales conversation   127

The elegant gift   130

PART II   **133**

The LinkedIn2Success Program   **134**

Case Studies   **136**

Bonuses   **149**

My Gift to You   **150**

About the Author   **152**

Foreword

When Adam Houlahan asked me to write the foreword to his book, *The LinkedIn Playbook*, my first reaction was to say no because I was so far from being any type of expert on the subject matter, or even a very disciplined user of LinkedIn. I was concerned that I would not add any degree of value.

Also, like many who will read this book, I am the owner of a busy small business and time is my greatest commodity. My business is a media and communications training and consultancy where managing issues and crises often arise. Clients can throw my daily time management out the window at any time, so I was nervous about my ability to give Adam the foreword he deserved.

But then I stopped and, selfishly, decided this request was just what I needed to finally tick off that long-standing item on my to-do list: learn LinkedIn properly.

I only wanted to learn from someone who knew what they were talking about, and who I felt confident would offer me current information to satisfy my business objective; namely, to learn the potential LinkedIn can offer as a strategic business tool to form or extend valuable relationships with potential and current clients, and/or develop further industry-profile and expert influence.

I am not writing this foreword because I have known Adam as a personal friend, or even as a professional colleague, for years. In fact, I don't really know Adam at all, but I feel like I do. And that's important.

I suppose the fact that he has amassed a social-media follower base in excess of 500,000 people globally across multiple networks in the last three years, and is a highly sought after social-media speaker internationally piqued my interest, but that wasn't all of it.

Adam's first book, *Social Media Secret Sauce*, was a hit and reached number one on Amazon. More importantly, Adam is someone who appears on your professional radar without you really knowing why. It is not through blatant, shameless self-promotion—a strategy that doesn't do anything to attract me, or most of my professional colleagues, and, thankfully, one that Adam actively disassociates from, as you will see when you read this book.

Adam Houlahan is one of those names you often hear talked about in small-business and entrepreneurial circles. His name just comes up again and again, and always in tones of approval, admiration and respect. It is that regular hearing of his name and obvious great reputation that makes you feel like you know him already and want to be involved with him.

So it was with eager eyes and a thirst for knowledge that I began to read *The LinkedIn Playbook*. I realised immediately the lack of real attention I had paid LinkedIn, a powerful lead and client generator, even though I had been on it for years. Well, I had really just whacked up some sort of cobbled-together profile and image.

Don't get me wrong. I have used LinkedIn regularly to find people who have contacted me, or I have wanted to connect with, and I have accepted many people's connection requests (don't ever send me a standard 'I'd like to add you to my professional network on LinkedIn message'—if you can't write me a proper message, call me by name or tell me why we should connect, you'll become pretty friendly with my delete button) but I had often wondered why everyone thought it was *such* an amazing platform.

Until reading Adam's book, I had never appreciated the breadth or the power of this platform. I never really knew why I was accepting people's requests to connect, or why I was inviting others to join my network.

I knew LinkedIn by reputation, and was aware that it was potentially the best B2B social platform, but Adam's book showed me *why*. It is a no-nonsense, practical, straight-to-the-point, step-by-step process to present yourself properly on LinkedIn (it makes you realise how second-rate your DIY profile job has been). But that's only the start, and the nuts and bolts. Adam shows you how to fix that in a flash.

The very tangible result of reading this book has been the penny dropping in two significant business areas. The first is the power of this platform over all others, and how savvy business people use it to build meaningful and valuable contacts and relationships. The net result of knowing how to play on LinkedIn properly, through Adam's *Playbook*, is that like-minded industry contacts, current clients, potential clients and peer associates will come to you to engage in an exchange of mutual, valuable knowledge. Or they will send others to you. The second area,

I believe, is the essence of influence, and the ultimate powerhouse of any person-to-person or service business.

So you will understand how horrified I was when, after doing one of Adam's simple influence-ranking exercises in the *Playbook*, I received a 'you rank in the lower 42 percent for profile views among professionals like you' result. Not happy!

As Adam says, 'LinkedIn is your fine-dining experience. It is ideal for those of us who are not as comfortable as others with narcissistic self-promotion.'

I changed many things on my LinkedIn as I read *The LinkedIn Playbook*, but it is a work in progress and I now know what I need to do. The best part is that I now know *why* I am going to do it. I have already seen the positive results of following Adam's advice, but now I know what I need to do to dive much deeper and achieve outstanding long-term benefit, and a significant ROI of my time.

This is Adam's powerful, value proposition.

That's a tick on my to-do list. Very satisfying. Thank you, Adam

Sam Elam
Founder and managing director of Media Manoeuvres
(www.mediamanoeuvres.com.au)

Introduction

Around the globe, the business world has experienced more upheaval in the last five years than during almost any other time in history. That upheaval and disruption has come not through recessions or government actions (or INaction!) The phenomenon is, of course, the internet.

The internet's impact has been, and continues to be, ubiquitous and profound. It has enabled what were once small or local industries and operators to reach out to the world. No longer can businesses define their competition by geographical boundaries or a level playing field in which all players are bound by the same rules.

Major disrupters such as Uber, Airbnb, Netflix and Alibaba are turning what were once considered A-grade business models into relics of the past. That impact will continue even more rapidly in the next five years. For many, it will mean an even tougher business environment. There will be ever more disrupters emerging, which will then become nimble and agile businesses dominating markets. There will be start-ups with savvy entrepreneurial backing becoming overnight successes.

LinkedIn has emerged as one of the powerhouses in the online space for business leads and sales; it now hosts almost half a billion of the world's movers and shakers. Yet this is not a book about the many features of LinkedIn. This is the *playbook*.

In part one of *The LinkedIn Playbook* I will outline exactly the step-by-step process that our clients are using right now with great success across the globe. I will give you the tools, scripts and processes you need before you start.

To begin, I will identify the seven key requirements that are the recipe (and hitherto secret ingredients) for success:

1 **Start with your *why*.** In the words of Simon Sinek, 'People don't buy what you do; they buy why you do it.' Your *why* underpins everything. Starting with your *why* is a critical step before you start creating your strategy.

2 **Social serving versus social selling.** We are constantly inundated with marketing concepts, and 'social selling' is one of the latest buzz phrases. *Social selling* is the process of developing relationships as part of the sales process. *Social serving* is taking this concept to another level and building relationships that take your contacts to customers who are desperate to work with you.

3 **You get what you give.** Imagine if every time someone connected with you on LinkedIn a person in need received the gift of education. By simply purchasing a copy of *The LinkedIn Playbook* you will make this happen. The gift of giving is a powerful concept utilised within the social-serving framework.

4 **The importance of your profile.** Getting your profile found is just the first step. Once your profile has been found, you have three seconds to convince this person to read more. When you

optimise your profile using the methodology outlined in *The LinkedIn Playbook*, your calls to action will be read a staggering 327 percent more often.

5 **Preparing for success.** To paraphrase Benjamin Franklin, if you fail to plan, you plan to fail. What you do before you start will make or break your success. You simply must get the pre-launch phase right. Planning every step ensures that you will convert more contacts to customers in the shortest possible time.

6 **The power of the law of reciprocity.** Social psychologists have known of this phenomenon for many years. Harnessing the law of reciprocity and implementing it into your social-serving strategy is one of the major factors to LinkedIn success.

7 **Creating pre-eminence.** Positioning yourself and your business as the leaders of your field, and creating trust, unlocks powerful forces, allowing you to handpick your clients, charge what you're worth and attract the premium A-grade team you've always desired.

In part two I have included case studies to give you some context across a number of industries. This will help you get a sense of the power of this process, and the potential it may have for you and your business.

Before we begin, grab a notebook and pen. You're about to create your own marketing playbook that will serve you faithfully in the years to come.

PART I

Chapter 1
START WITH WHY

There are four questions I always ask new clients:

1 Why do you want to use social media?
2 Why do you think LinkedIn is the best platform to use?
3 What is your company's *why*?
4 Why are you in business?

Same word, four very different answers required.

'll just step back one pace from these questions and explain the importance of these questions, and the importance of starting with *why*, not only in your social-media strategy but also in every facet of your business.

In 2009 Simon Sinek delivered one of the most poignant TED talks ever, which has been viewed by more than 1.7 million people. I highly recommend watching this presentation as soon as you finish reading this chapter. His talk is called 'Start with Why: How Great Leaders Inspire Action' (a simple search on YouTube will get you where you need to go).

The premise of Simon's presentation is very simple: people don't buy *what* you do; they buy *why* you do it.

The world's savviest brands embrace this concept, and once you understand the difference you will spot it daily in marketing campaigns on television, in print media and, of course, on social media. The concept is very simple: instead of telling your customers *what* you do and *how* you do it, first tell them *why* you do it, then *how* you do it and of course *what* you do.

Here is an example of *what* marketing:

At Maddison Hickey we work with you to develop a content strategy that will deliver your objectives. Social media is the tool that delivers quality traffic for your product and services. We utilise the best monitoring tools in the world to create comprehensive reports and insights you can rely on.

Creating high-quality content is what our teams thrive on and deliver on a daily basis. We also specialise in copywriting and growing your communities, with like-minded people just begging to become customers.

We are all well aware that social media is a powerful marketing medium, and that the key to success is integrating a marketing plan across multiple channels. This is what we do best. Maddison Hickey Social Media Services is your one-stop shop for social-media success. Call us today.

Here is how our company uses *why* marketing:

Web Traffic That Works is, you'll find, very different.

First, we have a real purpose: to help you create a powerful online presence that grows and accelerates your global footprint, so that together we can make a huge impact.

Second, we extend that impact by making sure that everything we do gives back in quite surprising ways, thanks to our lifetime partnership with Buy1GIVE1 (www.B1G1.com).

And in terms of how we do what we do, we understand there are three key challenges that our clients experience:

1 They struggle to get high-quality leads at an affordable cost.
2 They don't have the time to add social-media marketing to their daily tasks.
3 They know that creating a highly professional presence online over time is crucial, yet they also want immediate results.

We have designed a range of programs that will solve these frustrations:

- Targeted new leads every day
- Professional online presence your team can implement or which we will implement for you
- Return-on-investment that ensures our services are an asset and not an expense

The Web Traffic That Works program is an intensive 'deep dive'; a superb, results-producing methodology that creates a cutting-edge, lead-generation sales funnel for almost any industry.

Of course, there is no cookie-cutter program that suits every business; we know your business is as individual as you are. There are five programs to choose from, and each one is tailored to a specific need:

1 Social Media Done For You
2 Social Media Done With You
3 Social Media Do It Yourself
4 LinkedIn2Success Done For You
5 LinkedIn2Success Do It Yourself

Sound interesting? Email us today (clientdelight@webtrafficthatworks. com) and book an obligation-free Skype or phone chat so we can listen to your concerns, explore solutions and customise things specifically for you. We think you'll be genuinely surprised by what you discover.

Why do you want to use social media?

There are many different facets to social media, and it's easy to understand why so many people become confused and waste thousands, if not tens of thousands, of dollars in unsuccessful campaigns.

Over the past five years I have lived and breathed social media through our own social strategies and those of our clients. I want to let you in on a little pearl of wisdom from those years of constant evaluation: marketing your products, services and offers via paid social-media campaigns rarely delivers great results. Exceptions are when you're promoting deep discounts or end-of-season clearances, and the reason is that there's so much free high-value information on social media that we've become accustomed to thinking of the entire social-media platform as a free information service.

We will always use social media and the internet to research products and services we're interested in and comparing them with other offers. Therefore, unless your offer is the best value on the market today, many people might click on your advertisements but few will purchase.

If your reason for being active on social media is to promote your products and services, you will likely need a huge budget or you face some level of disappointment. Also, you should not waste your time reading the rest of this book; it is not for you.

On the other hand, if your *why* is to position your business, yourself or your brand as a market leader and you want to create the right strategy to do that, then keep reading.

Why do you think LinkedIn is the best platform for you?

If you're reading this book, clearly you believe LinkedIn will be able to deliver results for you. You should be considering LinkedIn if your market exists in the more than two hundred countries that have access to the platform. And if you can tick off one or more of the following points, then it's also the right platform for you:

- You need to create quality leads consistently.
- You would like a shorter, more direct sales funnel.
- You would like to maintain awareness of your services among your ideal customers.

- You would like your customers to find you when they're searching for the services you offer.
- You would like to attract people who will become long-term customers.
- You would like to be made aware of new potential clients automatically every day, based on your own criteria.
- You would like to have access to any or all of the above without a massive marketing budget.

If you can't tick off any of these options, then again you don't need to read any further. LinkedIn is not the platform for you, and that's fine. It's far better to know this in advance than waste time and energy in the wrong place. Another platform may well provide you with an ideal marketing medium.

What is your company's *why*?

Why are you in business? Amazingly, very few business owners can answer this question when first asked, or they default to the wrong answer. They might respond with 'To make money' or 'To provide a lifestyle for our family' or 'So I can put our children through private education, it's something I never had access to'. Don't get me wrong, these are noble objectives, but they are simply outcomes and not your *why*.

Understanding the importance of and knowing your *why* changes everything; it underpins everything you do from a marketing perspective.

It's the critical first step to success when you implement the strategies outlined in the *Playbook*.

I highly recommend that you complete the following two tasks before reading any further:

1 Watch the sixteen minutes of pure genius that is Simon Sinek's TED talk on YouTube: 'Start with Why: How Great Leaders Inspire Action'.

2 Complete this exercise until you are totally happy with the outcome. It's often not as easy as it seems. The exercise is of course to pen your *why*.

The exercise is best done with your team, because if they have some say in creating the *why* for your business they will feel a sense of pride and belief in it. It's highly unlikely you will nail this on the first attempt; if it were easy every company would have theirs now. Getting this right will place you ahead of the majority of your competitors and set you on the road to success using the methodologies you're about to uncover in the *Playbook*.

Here a few examples to give you some ideas:

Elite500

Run by Dr David Dugan, Elite500 is one of Australia's leading entrepreneur and business-coaching programs. David created an

E.L.I.T.E 5-step methodology combined with the Elite500 Mastermind mentoring group that specialises in co-piloting your business with you (for more information see www.daviddugan.com).

This is their *why* statement:

Why: We believe entrepreneurs are extraordinary. Everything we do nurtures that spirit and creates inspired results.

How: We do this by navigating with powerful simplicity, intelligent innovation and cultivating a connected community.

What: We deliver this through our elite business mentoring and coaching programs, and with our connected community of inspired business owners.'

Tayabali Tomlin

This multi-award-winning accounting firm based in Cheltenham, UK transforms the lives of entrepreneurs by providing clarity on their numbers, financial model and the fundamental economics of their business to achieve sustainable growth, superior profits and a plan for exit. They believe in thinking differently, challenging the status quo and transforming the lives of their clients, team, and those less fortunate around the world. One view of their *why* and you will understand why they are different and how they do things differently (for more information see www.tayabalitomlin.com).

Here is their *why* statement:

Why: We believe in thinking differently and in challenging the status quo. It's about creating an 'Oh!' in everything we do for you. We're passionate about business; we understand it, we get it. We love working out what makes businesses tick, and how we can improve them. And we get a kick out of seeing our clients have better lives because of us, whether that means more success, more wealth, or more time off. We believe in challenging our own team to excel in everything they do; above all in order to offer you outstanding levels of service. We also believe in changing lives: the lives of our clients, of their friends and families, and—through our charitable giving—of people right around the world.

How: Our experienced and high-calibre team are the best at what they do: employing their considerable expertise to help you take your business to the next level. We ask the right questions at the right times to offer innovative strategies for growth, along with cutting-edge tax planning and solutions to optimise your business.

What: Everything we do is intelligently and strategically focused on maximising your wealth. So whether you're looking for proactive and informed support to grow your profits, lower your tax bills, or manage your personal wealth, you'll find us right there with you.

Ceebeks Business Solutions

It seems the accounting world has embraced the *why* concept extremely well. Here is another example from Ceebeks Business Solutions in Australia, accountants in Warrnambool (South West Victoria, Australia) who have a focus on helping their customers improve their businesses to change their lives, and in turn improve the communities and lives of those less fortunate in the world.

Here is their *why* statement:

Why choose Ceebeks? We get up every morning to give young families in business solutions to improve their lifestyle. The rewards that follow allows our team (the 'fantastic four') to make small but powerful changes in our local community by volunteering two hours per week at Warrnambool and District Food Share; in our country with our regular blood and plasma donations at Red Cross; and in the lives of those less fortunate around the world with our lifetime partnership with Business for Good (www.blgl.com).

We love doing business with positive, fun-loving people we could see ourselves inviting over for a barbecue. Our culture revolves around loving what we do, so naturally we love having fun while we do it. Is that you?

You deserve advisors that are passionate, love what they do and are enthusiastic about making an IMPACT on your financial life. Don't you?

We are AWESOME at customer service and top of our game.

We are continually looking at tools, technologies, and education to become the best advisors in small business in South West Victoria. In fact, we won the international 2015 Change GPS Member Firm of the Year because of our early adoption of latest cloud-based technologies.

We work with families in business to make them more efficient, free up their time and develop a plan to achieve their goals.

If you want a simplified, growing business with clear directions to improve your family's lifestyle then you need to contact Ceebeks Business Solutions, the lifestyle accountants who IMPACT lives TODAY! www.ceebeks.com

Chapter 2

SEVEN ROOKIE MISTAKES YOU MUST AVOID

I know you're probably keen to race into the actual marketing program; however, this is a marathon and not a sprint. As with all elite sports, the race is often won or lost by the preparation that's done beforehand rather than the race itself. If you want to be an elite marketer, the same concept applies: the better you prepare before you start, the better your results are guaranteed to be.

That preparation also extends to the things you should *not* be doing, so in this chapter we're going to cover exactly that. Please keep in mind that while these rookie mistakes are relevant to LinkedIn, some apply to other social-media platforms as well.

The reason I've put this chapter at the front of the book is so you can rectify your current habits before you implement the *Playbook* methodology. If you're guilty of any of these little sins, stop now, and fix them today.

Content *not* to post

LinkedIn is the professionals' network and needs to be treated as such. Your connections on LinkedIn have no interest in your social life, your family, knowing what your dog is up to right now, or looking at the endless cat photos we see on other platforms. All that content (except the cat photos) has its place on Facebook, Instagram and Snapchat, but LinkedIn is not the place to share this type of information.

Think of LinkedIn as the place where you share information that serves your connections and followers. Everything you add to this platform should benefit your connections and followers in some way. Let me say that again: *everything you add to this platform should benefit your connections and followers in some way.*

The content you share should never be about you; it should consist of interesting articles your connections, customers or potential customers you have not yet connected with will find value in. You don't need to write the material yourself; it can be articles by other industry leaders as well. We'll get into that in more detail later, but from today make the decision not to post any more cat, dog or weekend barbecue photos on LinkedIn. Nothing at all would be better than this content.

Privacy settings

One of the biggest mistakes, and the easiest to fix, is having all or part of your profile set to Private. I suggest you remedy this right now, before you finish reading this chapter.

- Open your LinkedIn profile and check your settings. To do this, go to the Profile tab at the top of the page, and in the dropdown menu select Edit Profile. You'll see your profile URL below your profile image (mine looks like this: au.linkedin.com/in/adamhoulahan).
- Hover over the URL and click the settings link beside this URL and your settings will appear on the right-hand side.
- Click the radio button Make My Profile Visible to Everyone then tick every box below this.
- Click Save at the bottom and you're done.

We'll cover profile optimisation in an upcoming chapter, and once you have completed that process you will need to come back and check this section again. I'll remind you at the end of that chapter so it's not forgotten.

Adding your connections to your email database

Apart from being illegal, this is not a good idea. Just because someone has requested to connect with you, or you have requested to connect with them and they have accepted, this does not give you permission to add these people to any form of database. It does, however, give you permission to contact them directly through LinkedIn, and in an upcoming chapter we'll go through how you can ethically transfer them to your sales funnel.

More and more people I know are reporting as spam those emails that are being sent outside the LinkedIn platform, and other instances of being added to email databases without their permission. If you've done this in the past, I strongly urge you to remove these contacts as soon as you can. Going forward, you'll have a process whereby these new connections will gladly opt themselves into your databases, so you will have no need to use these unethical and illegal practices.

Over-posting updates and Pulse articles

Earlier we touched on the type of content you should be using; even if it's the right type of content you should use it sparingly. Unlike Twitter, where it's okay and actually good practice to tweet multiple times per day, on LinkedIn one to two updates per day and one article on Pulse (LinkIn's publisher platform) per week is more than enough.

Just to make it clear, an update is when you share a link to an article that resides either on LinkedIn or on other social-media platforms or blogs. You do this in the same way that you share an article on Facebook. Posts to Pulse are essentially blog posts you add directly to your LinkedIn profile in the same way you would add content to your blog.

If you add more content than this you run the risk of being viewed on LinkedIn as unprofessional, or worse, as a spammer. I'll repeat this idea many times throughout the *Playbook*. Before you do anything on LinkedIn, ask yourself this simple question: Would my connections or future customers get value from this?

Put another way, if you were connected with me on LinkedIn, would you want me sharing ten articles per day with you? Would you have the time or desire to consume that much content from me? Hopefully your answer is no. If you wouldn't want to receive this much content from someone else, your connections are also unlikely to want that much content from you.

Sharing a minimal volume of content means you can save your best stuff for LinkedIn. Think of it like inviting your best customers to a dinner party when you would bring out the best cutlery and dinner set, rather than a block party, where you would use paper plates and plastic cutlery. LinkedIn is your fine-dining experience; Facebook is for the block party.

Spamming your groups

In the past, many LinkedIn strategies have, and still do, promote being active in groups. Unlike second- and third-degree connections, with groups you can directly message members once you've been accepted into the group. But just because you can message group members it doesn't mean you *should* message them unless what you have to share serves them and not you.

Many of these strategies, if written prior to 2016, are in many ways redundant now. LinkedIn recently changed the rules with regard to how many messages you can send to group members. The limit is now fifteen messages per month to groups, and in my opinion it's a welcome limitation. That means fifteen messages across every group you are a member of and not each individual group.

Of course, if someone replies, the subsequent back-and-forth messages are not included, only the very first message in that thread. And if you don't use all fifteen messages they won't roll forward to the next month; your limit is always fifteen per month.

Just because you can now message group members only fifteen times each month, it still doesn't mean you should—not unless you have something of value for the recipient of that message. If you do, by all means send it to them. Groups still play a valuable role in the *Playbook* methodology, which we will cover in an upcoming chapter.

Self-promotion

Very soon we'll be getting into the concept of social serving. I'm looking forward to that chapter, and I know you will find it enlightening. I'll give you a small hint here: social serving has nothing to do with self-promotion. In fact, it is the exact opposite. I'm not suggesting that you shouldn't be promoting your products or services, but just that you do it in a specific way.

Until you've read this book in its entirety and have created the tools you'll be using, I highly recommend you stop all posts that promote you or your services. Just give it a little holiday until you're ready to do it the right way. Once you know the right way you'll never do that again on LinkedIn anyway.

Not personalising messages

LinkedIn allows you, and encourages you, to send messages to your connections on their birthdays or work anniversaries. This is like a post they share, a reply to an InMail (a purchasable LinkedIn service that allows you to message people who are not first-degree connections), or a recommendation you have requested. They even give you a default message for each instance. If you've been active on LinkedIn for a while you've probably been the recipient of one or another of these messages:

- *Happy birthday*
- *Congratulations on your anniversary*
- *Great post*
- *Quick reply (InMail)*
- *I would like to add you as a connection here in LinkedIn*

Sending one of these messages is about as engaging as handing someone a birthday card that simply says *Happy birthday* without any personal message from you. It's almost offensive to receive one of these messages, and possibly counterproductive, especially when you receive the same message two hundred times in a day, as I have.

The likelihood of the recipient feeling warm and thought of from these messages is highly unlikely. Think of the times you've received these messages on LinkedIn and how many times you've written back to that person thanking them for their kind thoughts. Almost never, I would bet.

Now think of contacting your connection in a way that makes them feel warm, appreciated or special, perhaps on their birthday or anniversary, or when they've shared something you found valuable. It's simple to do. Just take the twenty seconds required to change the impersonal default message to something different that actually means something (detailed examples that show how to do this are in a later chapter). I do this every day on LinkedIn, on average about fifty times per day, and I get a steady stream of people thanking me for thinking of them.

Of course they will also receive, depending on the size of their network, many of the impersonal versions as well, but I guarantee they will have forgotten who the sender was within minutes of reading the message, if they bothered to read the message at all. The golden rule is to always use a person's first name in the message. None of the default messages do this, so it's very easy to spot them.

There's another important reason for sending these messages, which we'll cover in an upcoming chapter. For now I suggest you just stop doing it, along with the other six rookie mistakes, until you have your complete *Playbook* methodology in place. Or, if you do continue to send messages of congratulations, do it in a more personal way.

So that's it for the rookie mistakes. Before you read on, make sure you've fixed up your privacy settings and changed any daily bad habits, even if it means that for now you don't post anything or send any messages.

Chapter 3
SOCIAL SERVING VERSUS SOCIAL SELLING

From Wikipedia: 'Social selling is the process of developing relationships as part of the sales process. Today this often takes place via social networks such as LinkedIn, Twitter, Facebook, and Pinterest, but it can take place either online or offline.'

What is social selling?

Potentially the buzz phrase of the year, social selling is everywhere we turn online. The concept has been in existence for many years; the revolution that is the internet allowed it to be reinvented with new tools to rapidly implement old ideas in powerful ways. Those tools, of course, are blogs, Facebook, Twitter, LinkedIn, and the myriad of other online resources in existence today. Just do a search for the phrase 'social selling' and you'll find over 350,000 results to choose from.

It seems everyone is racing to embrace this old concept in the new way. Don't get me wrong, it's a good concept, and at least it's based on developing a relationship with your audience as opposed to ramming your product or services down their throat. I'm a fan of any form of engagement that creates value first.

The basics of social selling are not difficult to embrace, and almost any business can implement it quickly. There are three basic steps to success:

1 **Be informed.** You must first understand who your customers are and what it is they're looking for. Researching these requirements has never been easier. In fact, LinkedIn is one of the best places to start because it delivers so much core information about your ideal clients through its almost resume-style format. (We'll cover this in more depth later in the *Playbook*.)

2 **Be real.** Creating trust and credibility is the underlying premise of social selling, and new connections will spot imposters very early in the process. Think of this in terms of attending a networking event. The person who never stops talking about themselves and their company will collect a lot of business cards, since people will usually hand one over as fast as they can to stop the person talking. That person's card will usually find its way to the trash as quickly as possible, and in a similar way your online connections will rapidly lose interest in you if you treat them in the same way. Don't be 'that person'.

3 **Create rapport.** Hopefully by now you will have watched Simon Sinek's TED talk and have embraced the concept of *why*. It's worth repeating: 'People don't buy what you do; they buy why you do it.' Creating trust, credibility and rapport is relationship-building 101. Engaging with your connections, and delivering genuine and relevant content over time is paramount to the social-selling concept.

So, the concept of social selling sounds great, doesn't it? And it is. That's why it's the buzz phrase right now, and social strategists worldwide are preaching its virtues. As with all good concepts, the innovators make all the mistakes, refine the process and then implement their newfound strategy. Then the early adopters jump on board well before the masses are even aware of the new way of doing things.

We're now in the latter phase of social selling, and it is now achieving acceptance. In other words, it has passed proof-of-concept stage and has mass-market acceptance.

If you're only just embracing social selling now, you're among the late majority who choose to sit back and wait until those who are behind new concepts can demonstrate many case studies and show examples of great success. And there's nothing wrong with that. Many successful companies that have stood the test of time operate in this way decade after decade. It's now a well documented and proven strategy that can deliver results.

So what are the innovators and early adopters doing right now?

What is social serving?

In the last chapter I suggested doing an online search for the term 'social selling'. If you did, I'm sure you would have found hundreds of thousands of links to choose from, including a Wikipedia definition. If you now do a search for 'social serving', first you will find there is no Wikipedia definition, and then you will see just a few thousand results linking to a real mishmash of unrelated articles.

The reason is simple: only the innovators are operating currently in this space, including myself. So let me give you my definition of what exactly social serving is: it is the process of existing for the sole purpose of solving the problems of your ideal clients and customers.

You business's *why* must be totally aligned with the needs of your clients. Your social-media strategy must also be aligned, and it must deliver a never-ending stream of high-value content and solutions. When you follow this methodology, the relationship-building process is what positions you and your company with pre-eminence, and creates a culture whereby your contacts and connections want to become customers and are desperate to work with you. (We'll cover the concept of pre-eminence in more detail soon.)

One of the key distinctions of social serving, when compared to social selling, is quite simply that it does not require a sales process. Social selling is still, at its core, a sales tool. When you create pre-eminence through social serving, the pre-sales conversation process that exists in social selling is replaced by a laser focus on delivering value and being valued by your connections. When they're ready to do business with you, they will come knocking on your door asking to become a client or customer.

LinkedIn is, by the nature of the way conversations take place, quite simply one of the best platforms available to create pre-eminence and practise social serving. This is what the *Playbook* provides: a step-by-step process to creating pre-eminence and implementing a social-serving strategy. The *Playbook* takes all of the great components of social selling and replaces the sales spin with higher-value methodologies that bypass these steps, delivering higher-value clients, and customers who are not shopping on price or comparing you to other service providers. They will come to you ready to do business, prepared to pay what your time or services are worth.

When you have pre-eminence and practise social serving, your sales conversations become very different. Not only will they be initiated by your connections, but also you will rarely be required to justify your pricing. This is due to the process you have adopted up to this point—of creating unwavering trust that you have the solutions, you have the track record, and your business and reputation is beyond question.

This is the holy grail of where every business aspires to be. This is why some businesses are talked about in the media and in networking conversations, and are known as the industry leaders. They attract the best clients, who are willing to pay a premium price to work with the industry heavyweights, leaving their competitors to squabble over the lower-value price-conscious leftovers. And of course they make more money.

So let's start your transformation now.

Chapter 4
CREATING PRE-EMINENCE

Let me begin this chapter by defining the term 'pre-eminence'. No, it's not the new buzzword of the day; the term simply means to attain a position of widely recognised importance. There have been many teachers of the concept of pre-eminence over the years, possibly none better than Jay Abraham. If you feel inclined to research this concept I highly recommend any of Jay's articles on the subject, many of which you can access for free online.

Personally, I am aligned with Jay's teachings on this subject; however, the strategies I'm about to outline relate specifically to creating a position of pre-eminence through LinkedIn, and dovetailing the concept with social serving.

As you will see, the two concepts align into a powerful methodology that few have yet mastered. Having said that, it's worth considering adopting these concepts across all of your business's activities in the future, keeping in mind that it will probably require a shift in the way you currently market yourself and your business on LinkedIn.

The majority of marketing still focuses on selling what it is you do. To create pre-eminence you will need to shift that focus to creating trust in your connections. They need to believe that you exist solely (in the business sense) to be their adviser in your area of expertise, and that you only have their best interests at heart. They need to feel that you value this position over and above the sales process; they need to feel that they are more than just a lead, a potential client or a number on your monthly KPI (key performance indicator) report.

You may also need to rethink the type of client you want to attract. If you currently value quantity of clients over quality, a shift will definitely be required. A person of pre-eminence is a rare thing, a diamond in the rough in the highly competitive marketplace we operate in today.

Pre-eminent leaders get to choose their clients, almost handpick them, if you will. A number of pre-eminent people I currently work with have a vetting process for new clients. People cannot just decide to be their clients; they interview potential clients to ensure they are a good fit for their business. We also do the same with all our clients now, and this isn't just a matter of being elitist or egotistical. The concept of vetting clients is about ensuring that you can give them the results they're looking for.

How often have you had a conversation with a colleague, in any industry, who has complained about having to work with a particular person or company? They usually end their rant with a statement like, 'Oh well, I just take their money every month. We all have to pay the bills, right?' If this is how you feel about your own clients, you're not serving their needs. If you're not serving their needs, you should not be working with them.

On those occasions where we decline to take on a client, we always give them a detailed explanation for our decision. Often the client is just not ready and needs to focus on other tasks, such as fixing their website, or having the systems and tools in place to serve the new clients we would be helping them connect with. We will often refer them to other specialists we know who can help them get these problems solved, and in this way we are still serving their best interest, even if it means not working with them at that time, or at all.

This is not to say that you should avoid leading a potential new client through a process of discovery, and even higher levels of trust building, including making sure they understand the value they would get from working with you. The subtle difference is that this process is initiated by the client; it's not part of a sales strategy whereby you entice thousands of leads to opt into your marketing funnel in the hope that a few will make the transition from clicking on a banner advertisement and work through the sales process that follows.

Some examples of businesses that would benefit from being pre-eminent are law firms that specialise in conveyancing. Traditional marketing tactics will, of course, reap results. The tough part of marketing to potential leads for these businesses is that no matter how good the offer, the lead needs to be looking for this service at the exact point in time it is advertised.

In other words, you could offer me free conveyancing for the next thirty days, but if I'm not looking to purchase a property in that timeframe then even a free service is of no interest to me. But by practising pre-eminence, these firms would be delivering a level of value to me over an extended period of time, and when I do need a conveyancing specialist I'm going to be highly likely to reach out and ask to become a client.

Another example would be a mechanical-repairs business. Once again, this could be a service I'm not in the market for right now, so all forms of traditional marketing would be wasted on me. It's also likely that at some point in the future I will have a need for a mechanic, and once again would be predisposed to reach out to the business that has been delivering great value to me over an extended period of time.

Essentially all service-based businesses—in fact, any form of consulting or marketing businesses—would benefit from adopting the pre-eminent methodology.

How to become pre-eminent

The art of positioning yourself with pre-eminence is to be seen by your co-workers, clients and peers as someone who provides great knowledge and practical advice in the niche area you operate within. The first step on the journey is to decide what exactly is the niche that you want to be pre-eminent in.

As in the previous example, if you're a lawyer then law is likely a little too wide. You would likely practise in a specific niche area within the law, for example litigation, corporate law or family law, to name just a few. Once you know your niche area of expertise, you will set about positioning yourself with pre-eminence in that niche, sharing as much high-quality advice and content as you can find or create relative to your niche. You would do this through LinkedIn specifically, but also on your blog and in as many other places as you can. (We'll go into this in more detail in the next chapter.)

By now you're likely thinking, well, if I'm never going to sell them anything what's the point of giving away so much valued information for free?

Taking our company as an example, you will rarely see advertising material promoting what it is we do. What we *do* promote is free content via blog articles, curated content, courses, podcast interviews, radio shows, and delivering keynote speeches around the world.

My last book, *Social Media Secret Sauce*, explains precisely how to build a highly targeted follower base through social media, yet many of our clients choose to have our teams do this for them. I'm happy to give away knowledge of the process we follow to anyone who wants it, but the reality is that most of the people who have read the book are not our ideal clients. Many of them share the content of my book and refer clients to us every week, essentially becoming advocates for us and playing an important role in our business model. It makes sense to treat them like royalty and provide them with as much information as possible to share and talk about.

The businesses and industry leaders we work with understand the higher value in what we offer. They understand this because we've been giving them loads of free advice and service for months, and in some cases years, before they contact us, wanting to work together. Or they come to know about us through advocates endorsing us by choice.

Essentially, our clients reach out to us because they have become comfortable with us over time, and trust, that essential ingredient for all successful relationships, has been established. If they've come to us via a referral, the trust resides between the new client and the referrer, but it can quickly be established with us.

Another shift you may need to make on the journey is in the way you view what it is you do: your products, your services and your business. Of course you need to have great products and services, and great business systems, too, but positioning yourself as having the greatest widget ever invented, or claiming that you extended your market share by X per cent last year is flawed marketing.

It's flawed in the sense that you will probably only hold that position in the marketplace for a certain period of time. It's flawed in the sense that it shows you value your position in the marketplace more than you do your client. It's also flawed in that your future clients don't really care anyway; they only care about who is the best service provider, and whether that provider will solve their problem today.

What you should be focusing on, and making your number-one priority always, is serving your client's needs. You should also be focusing on your team and ensuring they are empowered to serve your client's needs. If your team believe in the same outcomes you want to create for your clients, and if their *why* is aligned with your business's *why*, they will view what they do for your business and your clients in a meaningful way, and that will be visible to everyone they come in contact with.

Instil trust in your superior knowledge

Creating pre-eminence requires you to listen to the needs of your clients, but not to buy into their limitations. You are an authority on your subject, and you have a moral obligation to know more than your client knows. If you don't, then they don't need your services anyway.

Take a visit to the doctor, as an example. We expect that our doctor is always going to act in our best interest. Let's say I go to my doctor with a sore throat and a bad cough. I say that my friend has the same thing, and my friend's doctor said it was just the flu season and prescribed antibiotics. I then ask my doctor for a script for the same medication.

From my perspective, I may feel I'm dealing with the symptoms in a time- and cost-effective manner, based on some level of understanding of the cause of my ailment. My doctor, on the other hand, may have seen six other patients before me, all with the same symptoms, which match updates they're monitoring from government medical authorities. The doctor may also have a backlog of patients in the waiting room, most with similar ailments.

If my doctor was only interested in getting through all of the patients waiting today, and billing as many consults as possible, they could take on board my request, fill out the script and send me on my way. This would not be serving my needs, even though the doctor had done as I requested.

Looked at from the perspective of the doctor, they have studied medicine for many years, are up to date on current epidemics, and are highly experienced in their profession. Serving my needs would be to give me the best and most accurate diagnosis possible, and explain that to do this they need to take the time to run some tests, and go through a checklist to ensure that I'm being properly cared for. The doctor would meet my protestations of a lack of time, and my assurance that I know what's wrong with me, with resolve to do what they know is necessary to make a proper diagnosis. They would explain that it is their way or no way.

You need to take responsibility for your clients in the same way. You exist to serve their needs, to educate them as to what those needs are, and to stay resolute in the knowledge that close enough is never good enough, even when your client would be satisfied with close enough. Only then will you be treating them with the respect they deserve, and honouring your commitment to serve them to the highest level of your ability. You will also deepen their respect for you, and their desire to maintain a long-term relationship with you.

The same obligation applies when your client requests a service that is well above their needs right now. You obligation extends to educating them on why they don't need that option today, even though they may be convinced they do and are happy to hand over a large sum of money to you for providing it.

As an example, let's say you sell lawnmowers and a regular client arrives at your store. He says he was at his friend's house on the weekend, and his friend has this great new ride-on mower and can get the lawns into shape in no time.

Given your knowledge of this client's property (you've been dealing with him for a long time and have kept detailed notes about his home to better serve his needs) you know a ride-on mower is not what he needs. His yard has a steep slope, and a number of bushes and trees he would have to navigate around. You know there's a better option, which will give him the outcomes he's looking for, and it just happens to be one-tenth of the cost of the ride-on mower he has convinced himself to buy.

You would serve this client well by using your position of superior knowledge to educate him, and convince him to try another solution that would provide the outcome he needs, as opposed to the outcome he *believes* he wants. When he tries your solution and sees for himself that you were correct, and that you just happened to save him thousands of dollars, his trust in you will have deepened. He is never going to go to anyone else for advice or question the cost of your service again. He's also going to become your greatest advocate, spreading the word about your integrity and expertise, and effectively becoming a mobile one-person sales force that will bring in new clients at no cost to you.

The long-term value of networking

Hopefully by now you're getting the picture on how you could make some shifts to move towards pre-eminence. Effectively it starts before you've converted a lead to a client, when everything you do becomes steadfastly cemented in providing value and knowledge.

Most business owners I meet hate networking events, yet they see them as a necessary evil. I used to feel the same way and often avoided attending them. I hated to have *those* conversations, and I certainly hated to be sold to at the same time. That was until I understood the power of attending these events, which is to serve the needs of the others who are there.

I began to show genuine interest in other people's business problems, often offering to refer them to someone in my vast network who might be able to help. I started sharing my experience and expertise with as many people as possible, without focusing on pushing our business and services down their throats. At first this shift made attending these events quite enjoyable, but over time it also began to reap rewards through referrals, and attendees reaching out for assistance after the event, when the time was right for them.

Of course, I made it a priority to connect with the key people I met through LinkedIn, and to continue to provide free advice and services when asked. Sometimes it was when I felt that these people I was connecting with would benefit from an article I had written; at other times I would pass on something that someone else had written that solved problems.

Hopefully you will now see that becoming pre-eminent is all about solving problems, focusing on why you do what you do, creating value even before leads become clients, and positioning yourself as highly knowledgeable and influential in your industry. It's also about having meaningful conversations that provide the opportunity to give of yourself and your knowledge. This last point is one area where many people seem to struggle, falling back into those old habits of talking about themselves, their business and their services as their opening gambit in conversations.

Pre-eminent conversations focus on a theme more than a topic; they are about creating a lasting impression on the people you converse with. You need to decide what you wish to be remembered for in these conversations. You'll recall the earlier scenario, where you would not want to be remembered as 'that person' at events, the one who is remembered for all the wrong reasons.

Look at it as a simple reversal of this concept: instead of being remembered for the wrong reasons, ensure you're remembered for the right ones instead. There are many themes you could be remembered for: empathy, passion, energy, humour, respect, intelligence, class, wit, compassion ... the list is endless.

What you want to be remembered for should reflect your beliefs and personality. To put it simply, if you wish to be remembered as a caring person, show that you care about the people you converse with. If you want to be remembered as respectful, show respect for the people you converse with. If you want to be remembered for being passionate, show passion for your converser's story or needs.

When you demonstrate these qualities, you elevate yourself in people's minds and position yourself for future conversations.

Chapter 5
YOU GET WHAT YOU GIVE

Pre-eminence is, at its core, a team culture. It's about attracting the right people to your team and empowering them to join you on your journey, to believe in your *why*, and move beyond working for a pay cheque. This is certainly what you hope to achieve. Giving your team the tools, vision and permission to be part of something greater than them is one of the most valuable gifts you could ever bestow upon them.

The concept of giving in a business sense can mean, among other things, giving great value to your clients. Almost without exception your best clients, the ones who stay with you through thick and thin, will be the ones to whom you gave the most of yourself and your skills before they became clients.

One of the greatest gifts you can give anyone is your time, although of course this has to be in alignment with everything else you need to do. Your schedule should always allow time for you to speak at events, which could include speaking at your children's school on careers day, or at networking, industry or meet-up functions, or giving podcast or radio interviews.

Every week I allow some flexibility in my schedule to give freely of my time, and guess what? I've discovered that the more I give the more I will be asked to give.

When I first started on my entrepreneurial journey I openly solicited opportunities to share my knowledge. At networking functions I would make it known that I was open to speaking at events, offering people an open invitation to call on me whenever they needed. Today I'm fortunate enough to be asked to attend about as many events as I have time available, many of them in countries beyond Australia.

Speaking at events of almost any nature helps position you with pre-eminence, and always leads to conversations with attendees. As we covered in the last chapter, having these conversations is another opportunity to openly share your knowledge and best thinking. If done right, you will leave the impression that you desire to be remembered for.

To this day, rarely a week goes by that someone doesn't reach out to me, usually by email or through the contact form on my website, and the opening line of that correspondence is always along the lines of: *Hi, Adam, you may not remember me, but we met after the event* [last year, last month, last July]. The reasons people reach out vary, from requests for additional advice to offers for me to speak at a future event, and of course to become clients.

I must say I'm not a believer in the oft-repeated phrase, 'Give and expect nothing in return.' This might be a noble notion, yet the reality is that we *do* expect something in return for giving. I would rephrase this statement to: 'Give and expect nothing in return *right now*.'

We often give to people and get nothing in return, and that's fine, but realistically we do expect something in return from the overall concept of giving as much as we can. The return will come in many forms, ranging from satisfaction, gratitude, opportunity, referral, and of course financial returns. Giving should also be considered a mandatory part of any sales process.

In 2011 Google commissioned a study of buying behaviours and called this research 'The Zero Moment of Truth'. In a nutshell, The zero moment of truth refers to how many interactions you need to have with a prospective client before attempting to actually sell them anything. What Google found was that it requires seven hours, or eleven touch points, before a prospective client has gained enough trust in a seller to consider a purchase. Some argue that the timeframe has now been extended beyond seven hours, but regardless, giving freely of your time, resources and skill is simply a critical first step on the journey to building trust and creating sales.

Something I am a great believer in—and I have given many presentations on this concept alone—is the law of reciprocity. This law refers to the proven concept with regard to human nature that states that we are hardwired to return favours, often in a more generous manner than when we received the initial favour, so again it holds true that you get what you give. (We will cover the law of reciprocity in more detail soon.)

Creating impact

Something else I am a firm believer in is creating impact. Giving, in all of its forms, should always be underpinned by the mandate to create an impact on those you give to. The word *impact* is a powerful one.

It means to have a marked effect or influence. Pre-eminence therefore requires you to create impact in everything you do.

There are many ways to create impact. Richard Wiseman, a British psychologist, suggests there are fifteen ways to create positive impact in the presence of others:

1 Assume every person you meet is important, and treat them as such.

2 Shake hands strongly and firmly and, even better, say something positive while doing so.

3 Keep an open body posture, with your hands away from your face while speaking.

4 Stand up straight and tall, but not rigidly.

5 When speaking to a group, speak conversationally. Do not read from a script.

6 Take the time to remember people's names, and use them in conversation.

7 Look at the colour of people's eyes. They will notice the extra attention you're giving them.

8 Compliment people sincerely and freely.

9 Notice and acknowledge other people's strengths and accomplishments.

10 Use pauses while you speak to create emphasis.

11 Take care of your outside appearance; look your best.

12 Smile, ideally a little bit longer than the person you're looking at or listening to.

13 Hear the emotion in people's words, and respond to it.

14 Use positive body language. Maintain eye contact, briefly touch people on the upper arm, and move around while you speak.

15 Be genuinely interested in those around you. Ask them their opinions, enquire about their life and interests, listen and don't interrupt.

This is an excellent list of the habits of pre-eminent leaders. I highly recommend trying at least a few of these when you next attend a networking function. My personal favourites are numbers one to six. (If you would like to read more about Richard Wiseman's work, see https://en.wikipedia.org/wiki/Richard_Wiseman. The website is certainly an interesting read.)

On a deeper level, creating impact for your clients should be one of the cornerstones for doing what you do. Your role is to implement strategies that help your clients leave their mark on the world in a positive way.

Examples of excellence

A pre-eminent web designer will create impact through the beauty and functionality of the websites they create. A great example of this is Five By Five, a company owned by Jon Hollenberg, a good friend of mine. One look at their website and you just know these guys are going to go the extra distance and create something they're proud to put their name to—and you will be, too (www.fivebyfive.com.au; LinkedIn https://au.linkedin.com/in/jonhollenberg).

Jon Hollenberg is a sought-after speaker and author of the excellent book, *Love at First Site*. He is constantly attending events and giving his expertise to audiences all over Australia. We refer many of our clients to Jon, not because he is a personal friend but because we know the client will be looked after beyond their expectations. Simply put, we know the impact of Five By Five's websites.

Pre-eminent photographers don't just take photos; they create works of art. This attention to detail is impact in its most visual form. Another good friend of mine is one of Australia's most pre-eminent headshot photographers, Jason Malouin (https://au.linkedin.com/in/jasonmalouin). Jason owns The Portrait Store, a chain of photographic studios (www.portraitstore.com.au). Jason's work is unique; you can spot a Jason Malouin headshot on LinkedIn and know without a shadow of doubt that he was behind the camera. Jason's work creates incredible impact for his clients, and it is without question a status symbol to have your headshots created by Jason.

Jason is one of the most giving people I know when it comes to sharing knowledge, whether he's speaking at events or in general conversation. He's a great proponent of many of Richard Wiseman's teachings, and is always giving freely of his talents. Jason is involved in some incredible community projects, lending a hand in many ways.

There are many business coaches, who can be found in every city, covering almost every aspect of business you can imagine. Pre-eminent coaches, however, are much harder to find. Australia's Dr David Dugan, co-author of the bestselling book *Bullet Proof Business*, is one such coach.

You may recall the earlier reference to Elite500. Run by David and his team, this is one of the most impactful coaching programs you will ever find.

You cannot just join Elite500. The people and businesses that get accepted into this program achieve amazing results, and this is because David ensures that each person coming into the program has what it takes. He makes sure they are a good fit, both with him and the other members of his elite group.

Elite500's *why* statement: 'We believe entrepreneurs are extraordinary. Everything we do nurtures that spirit and creates inspired results. We do this by navigating with powerful simplicity and intelligent innovation, and by cultivating a connected community. We deliver this through our elite business-mentoring and -coaching programs, and with our connected community of inspired business owners.'

I highly recommend taking a look at David's LinkedIn profile, which is truly impactful (https://au.linkedin.com/in/daviddugan).

These are just some examples of the extraordinary entrepreneurs I have had the privilege to work with directly. They are all masters of their craft and pre-eminent leaders, and they are constantly creating impact above and beyond most businesses in their respective industries.

Your mission, if you choose to come on my journey to pre-eminence in your business, is to brainstorm with your team the way that you, too, can create impact in everything you do. This means every meeting you have, every proposal you write, and of course every client you work with. How much can you give of yourself and your business expecting nothing in return *right now*?

Charitable giving

One of the most important forms of giving is charitable giving. Its importance is due to the impact it creates: impact on the lives of the recipients of the giving, and impact, in a positive way, on our planet and how we take care of it.

Almost all pre-eminent leaders and companies have some form of giving program in their organisations. Generally speaking, they implement these policies only after many years on their business journey, usually on the premise that they cannot afford to practise charitable giving until their profits reach a level that affords them the ability to give some of it to worthy causes. Interestingly, most business owners I meet who are on their growth journey talk about the day they will be big enough to give back, so the concept of being involved in giving back seems second nature to most.

The facts around the level of charitable giving that takes place are staggering. In the United States alone, the National Philanthropic Trust has released the following statistics:

- Corporate giving contributes $17.77 billion annually
- Foundations contribute $53.7 billion annually
- 63 percent of high-net-worth donors cite 'giving back to the community' as the chief motivation in giving

You can read about all of the statistics they report at http://www.nptrust.org/philanthropic-resources/charitable-giving-statistics. What you will find is that most statistics seem to focus on the top end of town—the people and companies who can afford to give the most, and the largest charities that seem to be able to collect the most in donations.

We often hear in the news of celebrities and well-known leaders of business who have donated huge sums of money to causes of their choice. This is wonderful and I applaud them all for what they do in giving back. My only issue with these statistics and newsworthy events is that they instil in the other ninety-plus percent of people and businesses that giving back is reserved for the top end only. It creates the misguided belief that small and growing businesses cannot effectively have giving programs for their organisations.

I, too, used to be one of those people who wanted to implement an effective giving program but was under the same misguided belief that it was not an option for us. That was until March 2014, when I had the great fortune to meet Paul Dunn, chairman of the global giving initiative Buy1GIVE1, or B1G1, as it is also known (more on Paul and B1G1 to come).

Why is it important for small- and medium-sized businesses to have the opportunity to give back like the big corporations do? Quite simply, apart from the reality that it's an amazing experience to know that your business is making an important impact, either locally or around the world, your clients and future clients are profoundly impacted in a positive way when you do.

Giving back elevates your business in the eyes of your clients to a level above your competitors in terms of credibility, trust and reputation. Potential clients, who likely have a myriad of choices in service providers, are swayed in their decision-making processes when they are aware of your social soul.

The staggering statistic in the face of this irrefutable reality is that less than six percent of all businesses have a giving-back program in place. Not surprising, the majority of this six percent are the big corporations with deep pockets. It's highly likely that many thousands of small- and medium-sized businesses would also implement one if they knew how. It's also highly likely that if you do this now, you will be one of the very few businesses among your competitors, if any, with the opportunity of gaining this new level of credibility, trust and reputation among your current and future clients.

It's not virgin territory, but you can still be an early adopter of this very powerful shift in the way your business goes about its everyday activities.

Earlier I mentioned a chance meeting with Paul Dunn when we were speaking at the same conference. Fortunately my presentation was before Paul's. As anyone who has heard or seen one of Paul's presentations can attest, he is one of the world's most gifted presenters. I highly recommend that you watch Paul's four TEDx presentations. If you only watch one, make it 'The Power of Small'. It was exactly this presentation that Paul delivered after mine and it changed my life. The 'power of small' is a concept that marries everyday business activities with a giving-back program that is possibly more impactful than those of the large corporations and the value they receive from their programs.

It was on the back of Paul's presentation that I was able to create, almost overnight, an amazing giving-back program in our business that has, to date, created more than 400,000 giving impacts around the world. I did this through B1G1.

Buy one give one

B1G1 is not a charity in itself; it is much more than that, with over eight hundred projects around the world benefitting from the amazing work the organisation does and, staggeringly, around 100 million impacts created through their efforts. The projects accepted into the B1G1 family undergo an exhaustive due-diligence process by the board of B1G1, and, for varying reasons, very few get accepted into the program. It goes without saying that the ones that do make it into the fold are doing great things around the world.

B1G1 helps businesses just like yours and mine; businesses of every size in countries across the globe. They help our businesses in surprising ways, too, by helping to create measurable, long-lasting impacts; impacts that better the lives of many people and assist environmental causes to improve this planet we all inhabit.

B1G1 also helps business owners create real purpose, team spirit and better business practices. I have had the good fortune to meet or work with many of the B1G1 member businesses. They, like me, feel that their businesses are in better shape as a direct result of joining B1G1.

So, how is it done?

Start by imagining this: imagine if every time you bought a cup of coffee someone in need received access to life-saving water.

Or imagine that whenever you purchase a new book someone received the gift of sight. Or imagine that simply by buying your lunch today you fed someone else in need.

And imagine this: each new client in your business who requests your training services allows you to give the gift of education. Every item of clothing you sell provides a warm blanket to someone suffering the cold. Every machine you repair means someone gets a life-saving medical procedure they desperately need.

Put very simply (yet totally accurately), with B1G1 you're able to say, 'Every time you do business with us, something great happens.'

Let's take this one step further. What if you could create these impacts from as little as *one cent*? Can the coffee-shop owner afford to give one cent from every cup of coffee sold to ensure that someone receives life-saving water for a day? If you write or sell books, can you afford one cent from each sale to give someone the gift of sight? If you sell clothes, can you afford less than a dollar from the sale of a fifty-dollar dress to provide a warm blanket?

It sounds impossible, I know, and I would also be sceptical if I weren't already doing this. This is what B1G1 makes possible, and thousands of businesses are doing it every day in every way.

Now think about this? How do you think the clients of the businesses that practise this initiative through B1G1 feel about these coffee shops, law firms, mechanics, dentists, jewellers, fashion retailers, hairdressers, coaches, and the many thousands of other professions in the know? They love these businesses because the impacts created are directly related to the actions they take.

How much better do you think your morning coffee would taste if you knew you had provided safe drinking water for someone else? How likely would you be to walk past one coffee shop to spend your money with another that proudly states they're going to make this happen on your behalf?

This is 'the power of small', as Paul Dunn so eloquently shared in his TEDx talk. Small actions equal big impacts that every business of every size can participate in, not only to—most importantly—do great things around the world, but also to elevate their businesses in the eyes of themselves, their team and their customers.

Pre-eminent businesses and people give back. Smart businesses and people do it through the Global Giving Initiative that is B1G1 through the simplicity of joining and the simplicity of embedding giving into your everyday business activities.

Even for start-up businesses, it's inconceivable not to give back from the moment they open their doors—once they become aware of the power of giving through their business and how this can be directly related to rising success.

There's no need to wait until you have spent years building your business. You can start today. To find out more, visit B1G1.com.

Chapter 6
QUICK RECAP

So far we have covered the importance of creating a powerful *why* statement, and a culture in your business that supports that *why*. If you still haven't watched Simon Sinek's TEDx talk from chapter one, put this book down right now, grab your computer and watch it (search for 'Simon Sinek Start With Why').

We've also covered the seven rookie mistakes you must avoid on LinkedIn, so you've had some time to correct these before you start your new improved LinkedIn strategy.

Social serving versus social selling was next, which covered the subtle shifts that make marketing your business and yourself so much more enjoyable.

Probably my favourite chapter was next, which was on the value of becoming pre-eminent: positioning yourself and your business with pre-eminence.

Then we covered the many forms of giving that will make a huge impact in your business and everything you do.

These are all of the steps you need to consider before we move onto the LinkedIn site. Taking the time to work your way through the steps will ensure you have all of the necessary components in place once you get started.

You may recall the four questions we ask new clients before we discuss too much about what it is we do and how we can assist them in their marketing efforts:

1 Why do you want to use social media?
2 Why do you think LinkedIn is the best platform to use?
3 What is your company's why?
4 Why are you in business?

We ask these questions before discussing, in depth, the importance of having a sound business platform in place before attempting online marketing for a very good reason. I have had countless conversations with CEOs and business owners who all have horror stories about their first forays into online marketing. Many have learned huge lessons, usually at great financial cost.

We always look deeper—past the standard excuses like 'We partnered with the wrong firm' or 'They just didn't get what we were trying to do'—and it almost always comes down to the fact that these businesses are just not ready to attempt online marketing.

One of the biggest differentiators between the online world and the traditional sales model is how you build trust. This is infinitely more difficult to do online than in person or over the phone. If you cannot do it effectively in the traditional sense you have very little chance of doing it online.

All businesses are constantly looking for new sales channels, and to many the online option seems the obvious place to go, which it certainly is—if you get it right.

One of the biggest challenges I faced as CEO of companies I worked with was convincing boards of directors or stakeholders that in order to open new sales channels you have to do a massive amount of prior due diligence. You also need to have your own backyard in order before moving into new ones. With many companies, it was often the case that there were tens of thousands, and often hundreds of thousands, of dollars slipping through the existing sales channels because many of the topics we have covered in this book so far were not in place. These companies were often better off spending time and resources on sorting out these steps before looking for the golden goose online.

If you have picked up this book and started reading from this point on, which is where we start moving onto the mighty LinkedIn platform, you will have some degree of success if you implement the steps I'm about to outline. But if you take the time to work through what we have covered so far *before* moving onto the next steps, you will have far greater success.

It's all in the profile

LinkedIn, unlike most social-media platforms, is not the place for socialising and sharing with your friends and followers your weekend forays and, heaven forbid, those ubiquitous cat photos. LinkedIn is a *business* tool in every sense of the word and should be treated as such.

With almost five hundred million users on the platform, and two new profiles appearing every second, standing out from the rest of the

LinkedIn crowd is a must. One of the best ways of doing this is to have a truly exceptional profile.

If you scroll through your connections, or search within your industry, you will discover a vast difference in profile quality, ranging from embarrassing to very good. Occasionally you will come across truly exceptional profiles; you'll know as soon as you land on their pages that these people are at the top of their game.

The good news is that almost anyone can have, at the very least, a really great profile. For a truly exceptional version, you might need some assistance from a branding specialist who knows and understands LinkedIn, and if you wish to be connected with such people drop us an email at clientdelight@webtrafficthatworks.com.

Following the steps I outline in this chapter should at least get you up to the really great level, and this will put you in the top five percent of all profiles worldwide. You will be found in more searches, you will attract more of your ideal clients, and you will have the step-by-step processes to *engage-connect-convert* more leads into clients.

Once your profile is correctly optimised your name will rank very well with search engines, and in almost all cases your personal website as well if you have one, and your LinkedIn profile will compete for positions one and two in searches on your name. The importance of having a well-presented and optimised profile cannot be overstated; think of it in terms of the importance of your company or personal website. This is your opportunity to make a great first impression.

Think of online searches you've done in the past. When you've searched for a product or service you will have come across businesses with good functional websites, and others with less impressive websites. It's highly likely that you spent more time on the websites that were aesthetically pleasing and functional than the ones that were not. It's the same principle with LinkedIn: the profiles that present well and have great content get the attention they deserve. The rest fight for the limited attention span of impatient searchers and rarely generate any business for the owner.

Your LinkedIn profile is not your resume

Many of the profiles you see when you start searching look and read like resumes, and that's not surprising considering that LinkedIn started out catering specifically for this niche. But LinkedIn offers so much more now.

Another major differentiator between your resume and your LinkedIn profile when you're optimising for lead generation is the use of such titles as 'PHD Communications and Journalism' or 'Bachelor of Laws (LLB) combined degree' or, more specifically, where you use your titles if you have them. We'll cover this in more depth soon; the point I would like to stress here is the difference between a resume and lead generation on LinkedIn.

To continue using our lawyer as an example, if I was searching LinkedIn for a lawyer in a specific field of law, given that you are working for or own a law firm, I would take it on face value that you have a law degree. If you present this information in your name, summary or position description, you're using valuable real estate that would be far better used for more important content. There's a section specifically designed for adding this information, and by all means add it there.

One of the biggest mistakes you can make is to write your summary and position description in the third person. This is fine for resumes, or if you're specifically in job-search mode, but it's not okay for lead generation on LinkedIn. I still see so many profiles written in this way, and even worse, I still see LinkedIn training programs suggesting that people do this.

Instead of the seven rookie mistakes I outlined earlier, I should have made it eight, but since this is the profile section and I haven't even begun to discuss profile optimisation I'm happy to cover it here.

Let me repeat this important point: once we get started, be ready to write these sections in the *first person only*. By using first person, you're creating an immediate connection with anyone reading your profile for the first time. Third person, on the other hand, is impersonal and does nothing to create a desire in other people to want to get to know you, or read more about you and find out what it is you do.

Pronouns are often removed from resumes; many professional resume writers consider the words 'I' and 'me' redundant and will delete them. This is fine for a resume, but not for a LinkedIn profile. Always keep in mind that you want to connect with the people reading your profile in a meaningful way, so it's quite okay to use these pronouns.

Keyword optimisation

Keywords are critical on LinkedIn because the website's internal search engines use these to show your profile to people who are conducting searches based on specific terms. (There are also critical sections where you need to add them to your profile, which we will cover in depth very soon.)

Before you begin to optimise your profile, you'll need to do some research if you're not already familiar with the correct keywords for your industry. There are companies that will do this research for you if you're not sure what you should be looking for, and by all means reach out to them for assistance if you have the budget and don't feel it's something you can do well yourself.

For those who are willing to put in the effort, we'll now discuss a few pointers on what you should be looking for.

If you're not familiar with keywords and their role in the online world, they are almost magical little words or short phrases that search engines use to find content. If you spend time on social media in general you'll be familiar with hashtags, which are effectively keywords. By adding the hashtag symbol in front of your keyword you're asking the search engines of, say, Twitter to find all of the content on Twitter that contains that hashtag.

To relate that same principle to LinkedIn, its internal search engines deliver links to articles and profiles during searches. Think of this in terms of the search results you would want your profile to be found in. For me, some of the keywords are *LinkedIn, LinkedIn expert, social media, Facebook, Twitter, Instagram*.

One of your most important keywords is your job title. When someone is looking for your specific skill set, you want to ensure that you're in the running to be found. While it may sound obvious, making sure you have the correct keywords for your title is critical. One of the best ways to research these keywords is to do your own search on LinkedIn. Search now for the job titles you have listed. If your competitors are not showing up, then either you or they have the wrong keywords in their title.

You may also want to think about what exactly is your best job title or position description in LinkedIn terminology, and this doesn't necessarily have to match your business card or your email signature. Using a cool title like 'chief inspiration officer' might look great on your business card or email signature, but it won't help you be found on LinkedIn. You're not attempting to be found when you hand someone your card because you've already been found.

Similarly, traditional titles such as 'owner', 'CEO' or 'general manager' are pointless. If I were searching for an accountant I would search using that exact keyword: 'accountant'. I would not search for a general manager of an accounting firm. This is a high-density keyword area, so you could make your position description 'general manager and accountant'.

Getting the title wrong can be a big blow to your visibility. There can be subtle variations on the terms people use to search, but I've found that the most effective way of researching the most commonly searched-for titles is to use a free tool by a job site called Indeed (you can find the tool at www.indeed.com/jobtrends). All you need to do is add in any variations for a specific job title and the program will show you how many job listings have been used to find those positions. You can then use the most popular version.

As an example, use my position description and variations thereof, and you will see how I decided on my title. One tip: if, like mine, your title contains more than one word ensure you place inverted commas at the beginning and end. In my industry many people describe themselves as 'social media expert', 'social media specialist' or 'social media strategist'. If you place all three of these terms into the program you'll see that by a wide margin there are more companies using the term 'social media strategist' than anything else.

LinkedIn will also use specific words within your profile to deliver links to your profile in searches. These are your secondary keywords and are highly valuable as well. You can and should use these to some degree in various areas of your profile, and one of the most important is the skills endorsement. LinkedIn places quite a degree of importance on someone's endorsement of you for these skills and then delivers your profile in searches based on them. So don't think of these words as skills; think of them as keywords you wish to be found for.

You can have up to fifty skills, so you have plenty of scope to come up with a great list here. This is also where you can add, as secondary keywords, the variations you didn't use in your main-position descriptions.

So take the time now to do some research and decide on your best position description and secondary keyword list. You'll want to have this on hand when you start to update your profile.

Pictures speak a thousand words

This is not a rookie mistake; it is made by millions of LinkedIn users, regardless of how long they've been using the platform. There are two highly visual areas of your profile that deserve special attention: your profile image and your background image.

Your profile image should be a headshot of yourself, and no, a selfie from your mobile phone is not going to do you justice. This is the first impression of you someone is going to get when they first hit your profile. It's a well-known fact that we're predisposed to look at the image of a person before we look at anything else, regardless of whether it's a LinkedIn profile, a website or a blog. Heat-mapping technology, although not available on LinkedIn, has shown that this is where our eyes always gravitate to when we land on any page containing images.

Considering, also, that you're about to get more profile views than ever before, it makes a lot of sense to ensure you use the best-quality image possible. Using a ten-year-old version of you is not a great idea either. You're also going to have more face-to-face meetings and more Skype calls than you have up to now. If you look significantly different to your profile image you will plant doubt in the minds of potential new clients as soon as you meet.

Update your profile image at least every two years. If you suddenly decide to shave your head or dye your hair orange, it's best to update your image if that's a permanent new look for you.

We send all the clients we work with on profile optimisation and LinkedIn strategies to a professional photographer to have a truly great image produced. You can get this done for just a few hundred dollars. If you live in Australia I highly recommend Portrait Store, which can be found in most major cities (www.portraitstore.com.au). If you cannot use Portrait Store, most other professional photographers will do a much better job than you or I ever could. If your budget doesn't stretch to a professional photographer right now, don't let that stop you creating a good image for your LinkedIn page.

Here are five simple tips on producing a good headshot for LinkedIn:

1 Ensure the background is very plain, with no trees, walls or pictures to compete for people's attention. You want to make sure they focus on you.

2 Have the shot taken in a well-lit area.

3 Ask the person taking your photo to focus on your eyes.

4 Make sure your eyes are above the middle of the image. If necessary, crop out the top of your head to ensure your eyes are in the best position.

5 Keep it a real headshot. This means keeping the view either directly on your head, or on your head and shoulders and no more.

Once you have the best headshot you can produce, you'll need to size it correctly to fit your LinkedIn profile. The correct size is 500 x 500 pixels. You can easily do this yourself using free software like Pic Monkey (www.picmonkey.com).

The background image is much tougher to get right, and unless you have some skills in graphic design this might also be something you want to outsource to professionals. You can still have this done very cheaply, possibly for as little as twenty dollars, through sites like Fiverr (www.fiverr.com). Just ensure you select someone who is familiar with making these images for LinkedIn profiles, and it's a good idea to ask the person doing the job to send you samples of their previous work.

The correct size for the background image is 1400 x 425 pixels. Make sure the person who is creating the image for you works with these dimensions and supplies you with the completed image at the right size ready to upload to your profile.

If you want to save time, LinkedIn does provide some stock images that are suitable for backgrounds. Just hover over the area above your profile image and you'll be given a range of images to choose from. It's better to use one of these than have nothing at all. (With any LinkedIn profile, there is a section in the middle of the header that is not removable. This section will appear on top of any image you upload, so you need to take this into account when formatting your image by leaving the area blank.)

Optimising your profile

Now it's time to start getting your profile into shape. The first step is to go into your profile and turn off the notifications to your network. You'll likely be making a lot of changes, and if you leave this on every change you make will be broadcast to your followers.

To turn off your notifications, go to the Profile tab and select Edit Profile from the dropdown menu. On the right-hand side, beneath the Profile Strength indicator, you'll see Notify Your Network. Make sure you switch this off. I suggest leaving it off until you fully complete your profile-optimisation tasks. Just remember to turn it back on once you have finished.

We've already covered your background image and profile images. Now we're going to work our way down your profile and go into some depth on each section. The sections may not be in the exact order shown here since many are configurable with regard to where you place them on your profile.

Professional headline

You have 120 characters to play with in this section, so use them well. This is the section directly below your name. On the right-hand side click the Edit tab and this will allow you to input your chosen text. LinkedIn uses the data you add here in the form of keywords. There are two ways you can structure this area:

1 **Use all keywords, separated by icons.** This is how I do mine. Here is an example of another client who has used this format exceptionally well:

   *Digital marketing *Author *Speaker *Small-business mentor *Web design *Social media *SEO *Blogging *Strategy *Content

   I highly recommend you create this in a Word document first before uploading to this section of your profile. Keep in mind that the 120-character limit includes spaces and icons.

63

The icons give your profile more aesthetic balance, and you can use any icons that resonate with you.

2 **Write a flowing sentence that includes your main keywords.** Here is another example:

*Digital marketing expert and bestselling author
Keynote speaker focusing on SEO, blogging and web design*

Either of these options is fine. The important thing is to include your best keywords, ensuring they are words you would like to be found under in organic searches.

Country and industry

Selecting the country you live in should be easy enough to do correctly, but deciding on the industry you work in may not be so straightforward. LinkedIn has a specific set of industries in alphabetical order in a dropdown menu and you can choose from this list only. You may need to do a little research in the option you think best fits you. Type this term into the search bar and see who else comes up in the same field. If none of your colleagues or competitors show up you might need to reconsider your choice. Alternatively, search for your colleagues and see which industry they have chosen.

Profile URL

By default, LinkedIn will apply an obscure URL to your page, and you can edit the last section of this to something more memorable and useful when you choose to share your link. To edit the URL, when you're in Edit Profile hover over the URL and click on the settings symbol that appears. Your public profile will now appear. On the right-hand side you will see Your Public Profile URL. Click the pencil icon to the right of the URL and you can now edit this area, adding your name.

Every URL must be unique, so LinkedIn will provide some options if someone else has already registered your first choice. You can either choose one of these or attempt another version of your own. Once you've decided on an available option, click Save and you're ready to move onto the next section.

Privacy settings

Hover the cursor over your photo in the top-right corner of your home page and select Privacy & Settings. Click Edit Your Public Profile and set your profile to Make my Public Profile Visible to Everyone. Tick every section below to make these visible as well. If you don't have them visible, many people who might have connected with you after coming across your profile may choose not to simply because they don't have all the necessary information to make that decision.

You're doing this now because you're in this area at the moment, but you should come back to it again as your very last task and check it again. As you make more areas of your profile active you might find there are additional sections to make visible later. Once you've completed your profile optimisation you should never have to come back to this section again.

Contact information

Go back to the Profile tab and select Edit Profile. Contact Information is directly to the right of the URL. Click on this to open it up for editing and you'll see four options for adding additional information:

- Email address
- Phone
- IM
- Address

These options will only ever be visible to your first-level connections. You should complete this section with as many details as you're comfortable sharing with your connections.

Below this is an additional section headed Visible to Everyone on LinkedIn:

- Twitter
- WeChat
- Websites

Again, you should give as much information as you're comfortable sharing. You can have up to two Twitter handles. You might add a personal one and a company one. If you use WeChat, you could add this as well.

You can add up to three websites, and you can customise the description beside the website addresses if you decide not to choose the standard options offered. Choose Other and a new field will appear, allowing you to describe your websites as you see fit. You can use up to thirty characters here, and 250 characters for your website itself.

Once you've completed this area, click Save.

There are three other sections within your main profile frame. These are your current job roles, your previous job roles and your education. These areas are automatically populated when you complete the next sections of your profile.

Summary

Although the Summary is an optional addition to your profile, it should be included and placed at the very top of your profile. You have 2000 characters to work with in the Summary. All the sections we've covered so far are very important to get right, but this will probably be the most difficult to complete. This is your opportunity to get somebody interested in you. If you lose people here, it is highly unlikely they will read or interact any further.

You need to cover a number of points, and the challenge will be to do so in 2,000 characters or less. The format I outline below has proven itself hundreds of times over, across dozens of industries, countries and even languages. The points, in order:

- Your name
- Your claim to fame
- Your insight
- The result you will deliver
- Your experience

- The problems you will solve
- How you solve these problems
- Your *why* (this is your personal *why*; what gets you up every morning, excited and energised)
- Call to action

Here is what a completed version using this methodology might look like:

Hi, Adam Houlahan here, author of *Social Media Secret Sauce* and CEO of Web Traffic That Works. I wish I had a dollar for every time business owners I meet said they just don't get social media. What's the return-on-investment, they ask. Well, it's simple: *YOU GET TO STAY IN BUSINESS*

I work with business owners and entrepreneurs to gain real influence and credibility through social media. I do this by designing game-changing strategies that deliver quality leads from your ideal clients, and an online presence that positions you as the industry expert.

Having owned and run six companies myself, I was well aware of the difficulties businesses face in obtaining a powerful integrated social media presence, especially on LinkedIn. I realised there were three key problems we all experience:

1 We struggle to get high-quality leads at an affordable cost.

2 We don't have the time to add social-media marketing to our daily tasks.

3 We know that creating a highly professional presence online over time is crucial, yet we also want immediate results.

To solve these frustrations I designed a program that creates solutions:

- Targeted new leads every day
- Professional presence online your team can implement or which we will implement for you
- Return-on-investment that ensures our services are an asset rather than an expense

I believe every business has the power to change lives by giving back through its everyday business activities. My personal goal for this year is to positively impact the lives of 200,000 people in need. Doing this with my clients is a simple yet powerful way of putting this belief into action. Together we can make a huge impact.

Want to stay in touch, or just get access to the *FREE* information I share every day? Then click the blue Connect button above. If you would like a *FREE* copy of my LinkedIn Optimisation course, click the link below. For more information about our new service, Web Traffic That Works, click the link on the right.

Now here is the same summary broken down into each component. Hopefully it will seem a little less daunting when each part is looked at separately:

- Name and claim to fame:
  Hi, Adam Houlahan here, author of *Social Media Secret Sauce* and CEO of Web Traffic That Works.
- My insight:
  I wish I had a dollar for every time business owners I meet said they just don't get social media. What is the return-on-investment, they ask. Well, it's simple:
  YOU GET TO STAY IN BUSINESS
- The result I will deliver:
  I work with business owners and entrepreneurs to gain real influence and credibility through social media. I do this by designing game-changing strategies that deliver quality leads from your ideal clients, and an online presence that positions you as the industry expert.
- My experience:
  Having owned and run six companies myself, I was well aware of the difficulties businesses face in obtaining a powerful integrated social media presence, especially on LinkedIn.
- The problems I solve:
  I realised there were three key problems we all experience:
  1 We struggle to get high-quality leads at an affordable cost.
  2 We don't have the time to add social-media marketing to our daily tasks.

3 We know that creating a highly professional presence online over time is crucial, yet we also want immediate results.

- How I solve these problems:

    To solve these frustrations I designed a program that creates solutions:

    - Targeted new leads every day
    - Professional presence online that your team can implement or that we will implement for you
    - Return-on-investment that ensures our services are an asset rather than an expense
    - My *why*: I believe every business has the power to change lives by giving back through its everyday business activities. My personal goal for this year is to positively impact the lives of 200,000 people in need. Doing this with my clients is a simple yet powerful way of putting this belief into action. Together we can make a huge impact.
    - Call to action: Want to stay in touch, or just get access to the *FREE* information I share every day? Then click the blue Connect button above. If you would like a *FREE* copy of my LinkedIn Optimisation course, click the link below. For more information about our new service, Web Traffic That Works, click the link on the right.

If you go to my profile on LinkedIn, you'll see professionally produced banner ads with clickable links to the two landing pages described above. Again, this is something that can be created for you at low cost through sites like Fiverr. The rest of the information has direct links to my interviews or media appearances. If you have content like this it will add huge credibility to your profile, so use it if you have it.

Now it's your turn. Again, I suggest you do this in a Word document first, using icons for aesthetic appeal and checking to see how many characters you've used before you upload it to your profile. The 2,000-character limit includes spaces and icons. Even a line separating paragraphs counts as a character.

Experience

You have 2000 characters to work with. This is the section that shows the current and previous positions you have held. The only one I would suggest using this methodology for is your current position. You do have 2,000 characters available again, but the format of this section is quite different. Whereas the summary covered insights into yourself and your personal *why*, plus more, here you'll cover fewer points—four, in fact—but we will now go a little deeper in our explanation of these topics.

The topics to use:

- Why (this is your business *why*: why does your business exist?)
- How
- What
- Call to action

In this section you also have a title, and in an earlier section we covered how you should choose your title. This is also an area LinkedIn considers as keywords, so choose your title carefully. Here is my completed version in its entirety:

Social Media Strategist and LinkedIn Expert
(You can use up to 100 characters for this; note that I haven't used my professional title of CEO.)

Web Traffic That Works is, you'll find, very different. First, we have a real purpose: to help you create a powerful online presence that grows and accelerates your global footprint so that together we can make a huge impact. Second, we extend that impact by making sure that everything we do gives back in quite surprising ways, thanks to our lifetime partnership with Buy1GIVE1 (www.B1G1.com).

And in terms of how we do what we do, we understand that our clients experience three key challenges:

1 They struggle to get high-quality leads at an affordable cost.
2 They don't have the time to add social-media marketing to their daily tasks.
3 They know that creating a highly professional presence online over time is crucial, but they also want immediate results.

We have designed a range of programs that will solve these frustrations:

- Targeted new leads every day
- Professional online presence your team can implement or which we will implement for you
- Return-on-investment that ensures our services are an asset and not an expense

The Web Traffic That Works program is an intensive 'deep dive'; a superb, results-producing methodology that creates a cutting-edge, lead-generation sales funnel for almost any industry.

Of course, there is no cookie-cutter program that suits every business; we know your business is as individual as you are. There are five programs to choose from, and each one is tailored to a specific need:

1 Social Media Done For You
2 Social Media Done With You
3 Social Media Do It Yourself
4 LinkedIn2Success Done For You
5 LinkedIn2Success Do It Yourself

Sound interesting? Email us today (clientdelight@ webtrafficthatworks.com) and book an obligation-free Skype or phone chat so we can listen to your concerns, explore solutions and customise things specifically for you. We think you'll be genuinely surprised by what you discover.

Now here it is broken down into the four components:

1 **Why.** Web Traffic That Works is, you'll find, very different. First, we have a real purpose: to help you create a powerful online presence that grows and accelerates your global footprint so that together we can make a huge impact. Second, we extend that impact by making sure that everything we do gives back in quite surprising ways, thanks to our lifetime partnership with Buy1GIVE1 (ww.B1G1.com).

2 **How.** And in terms of how we do what we do, we understand that our clients experience three key challenges:

   1. They struggle to get high-quality leads at an affordable cost.
   2. They don't have the time to add social-media marketing to their daily tasks.
   3. They know that creating a highly professional presence online over time is crucial, yet they also want immediate results.

3 **What.** We have designed a range of programs that will solve these frustrations:

   ◆ Targeted new leads every day
   ◆ Professional online presence your team can implement or which we will implement for you
   ◆ Return-on-investment that ensures our services are an asset and not an expense

   The Web Traffic That Works program is an intensive 'deep dive'; a superb, results-producing methodology that creates a cutting-edge, lead-generation sales funnel for almost any industry.

Of course, there is no cookie-cutter program that suits every business; we know your business is as individual as you are. There are five programs to choose from, and each one is tailored to a specific need:

1. Social Media Done For You
2. Social Media Done With You
3. Social Media Do It Yourself
4. LinkedIn2Success Done For You
5. LinkedIn2Success Do It Yourself

4 **Call to action.** Sound interesting? Email us today (clientdelight@ webtrafficthatworks.com) and book an obligation-free Skype or phone chat so we can listen to your concerns, explore solutions and customise things specifically for you. We think you'll be genuinely surprised by what you discover.

You may find that some of this section overlaps the information given in your summary and that's quite okay as it is reiterating the important points.

Now it's your turn to create a compelling position description in 2,000 characters or less. You can add further links under this section if you have the content to use, but the summary is by far the most important area to use them if you do not have enough.

Skills and endorsements

You can have up to fifty skills in this section and I highly recommend you choose all fifty. If you don't, LinkedIn will choose, with some

76

degree of random relevance, additional ones for you. You can always remove these, but you will find it simpler to select your own list rather than leaving it to the mercy of the random additions.

The keywords you've used up until now should all be represented in this list, and they should be in order of their value to you, from highest to lowest. From there, add additional relevant skills to fill the fifty available. If you're struggling to come up with fifty, it's quite okay to put in as many as you have and add to this as you progress. This section should be placed as high up as possible on your profile, just below your summary or just below your experience. This will make it as easy as possible for connections to endorse you for these skills.

Language

This is one of the optional fields you can add from the overall list, which may not be activated on your profile right now. If you cannot see this section, go to the top of your profile and immediately below your URL you will see the area called Add a Section to Your Profile. Open the clickable tab View More and you will find the language section.

If your main language is English you should still add it here, as LinkedIn will use your languages in making your profile visible in some searches. If you speak other languages, even with limited proficiency, add them here too.

Additional info

This is again a keyword area, although of less importance than the main areas at the top of your profile. You can use some keywords here if you choose to, as well as specific interests you may wish to share with your connections.

Advice for contacting

You must add this section, which will appear in the above area under Additional Info. Be very clear and descriptive in offering your contact options. It could be through your website, through your PA or any other options you choose.

Education

You must complete this section in your profile. Many people leave this blank, possibly due to not having a degree or similar. LinkedIn will consider your profile incomplete if you don't add something here, and this means you'll show up in fewer searches. You can also add links to your school, university and other training institutions if they have a presence on LinkedIn.

Recommendations

Other than a video testimonial, there's no better validation of your pre-eminence than a LinkedIn recommendation. When you have conversations with people you would like to receive a recommendation from, don't be afraid to request one. You might be surprised at how many people will do this if you just ask. Make it easy for them and send them the link to do this for you. To send them the link, go to your profile, and specifically to Recommendations. At the bottom of this section, click on Ask To Be Recommended and follow the simple process from there.

Ensure you send a personalised request, just like everything else you do on LinkedIn from now on. You may also find you'll receive offers to swap recommendations from connections that you're not genuinely doing business with. While having recommendations is important, it's far better to have a few genuine recommendations than many insincere or even false ones. There's no magic number—other than zero. This should be a work in progress from now forward.

Groups

You can join up to a hundred groups, and the ideal ones to join are those that contain your ideal clients. These will be more valuable to you than groups that have interests specific to you. As an example, you may be an avid sailor, but unless other sailors are your ideal clients, groups focused on sailing are not the ones to join. You can go ahead and join interest groups—with the limit now increased to a hundred you can certainly be in both—but for the purposes of generating leads the groups to join are those I have outlined.

This should again be a work in progress because there are limits to how many outstanding requests to join groups you can have. Currently it is ten at any one time. You will find that some allow you to join quite quickly while others will be slow for many reasons, including the moderator not attending to requests regularly, or the moderator not taking the time to check into your profile to see if you are a good fit.

Following

There are now many influencers on LinkedIn that are well worth following. These people may not readily accept your connection request, but by following their profile you can have access to their posts and status updates, which could be worth reading. To add these people to your following list, just search for them, and once you're on their profile you will have the option of following them.

Alternatively, for inspiration you could take a look at some of your connections' profiles. There are a number of such pre-eminent people in this section of my profile that you can view any time.

Profile rating

Depending on how well you have followed the above instructions, LinkedIn will now give your profile a rating. If you have implemented all of the non-optional steps I've outlined you should have the highest ranking of All Star. To see your ranking, go to your profile page and on the right-hand side you will see Profile Strength. LinkedIn uses this indicator to gauge how complete your profile is. You must get your profile to the All Star level. There are five levels:

1 Beginner
2 Intermediate
3 Advanced

4 Expert

5 All Star

The only one you need worry about is All Star; anything below this means you still have some work to do. If you've followed all of the steps above and are still sitting below All Star, the only reason could be that you have less than fifty connections. This is the only other requirement beyond the steps I have given you.

Optional sections you can include

It's necessary to implement all of the above sections in a professional manner before your profile is complete. However, there are also a number of additions you can make to your profile that are totally optional. If you have good content to add via these options, by all means add them. It's as simple as a one-click process and these sections will activate to your profile.

You can find the full list of optional additions by going to your profile in edit mode. Just below your main profile box you'll see the dropdown option Add a Section to Your Profile. Open this up and select any of the options you deem relevant. A word of caution: don't add sections just for the sake of it, but only if they will enhance your credibility.

Finally, once you've completed all of your profile optimisation don't forget to turn your notifications back on. (Go to the Profile tab and select Edit Profile from the dropdown box. Beneath the Profile Strength Indicator, you'll see Notify Your Network. Switch this back on.) It will assist you if your connections and followers are notified of your posts, status updates, anniversaries, and so on.

LinkedIn character limits

Below are some useful details you may wish to keep on hand while updating your profile. These are the maximum characters allowed in each section you will be using.

Name 60
Professional headline 120
Summary 2,000

Contact Information
Website description 30
Website URL 250
Phone number 25
Instant message 25
Address 1,000

Experience
Company name 100
Job title 100
Position description 2,000
Status updates 700

Chapter 7
PREPARE FOR SUCCESS

Once your profile is optimised correctly it will be speaking to your ideal clients in a way they understand and are looking for. In other words, it will be acknowledging their problems and offering solutions. And once you have every section of your profile completed to All Star level you'll find that this alone will be enough to get you noticed and engagements happening.

One of our clients we assisted with this process contacted me recently, and this is what she said: 'I updated my details in LinkedIn as well as my photo. I'd never received one lead from LinkedIn prior to these changes, but yesterday I received a message asking for a phone call today. I called the lady and I'm very likely to get a sale out of it. Although it's only a small sale, it's a start.'

I asked the client how she found me, and she said she was looking at someone else and my name popped up as a second connection. She saw the photo and my description, and thought I would be a better option than the one she was looking at so she contacted me instead.

This is not an uncommon occurrence. At this point in the process your own profile will already be better presented than more than ninety percent of the other profiles you see on LinkedIn. It makes sense that people will start to reach out to you; they know you have the solutions to their problems.

This is the opportune time to put in place the final plans for success.

Critical drivers and key-performance indicators

Identifying and monitoring the key critical drivers of your business is a standard tool any business coach would put in place. It's also important to identify and monitor these same drivers for your marketing campaigns, which essentially form a subset of your business's overall drivers.

A critical driver is something that has a major impact on the performance of your specific business, and in this instance campaign. A whole range of internal and external factors can affect the success of everything you do. The secret is to focus on a handful of the critical drivers that reflect the performance and progress of your campaign. They must be measurable; they can be compared to a starting point or outcome you're looking to achieve.

Key performance indicators (KPI) are an evaluation of the success of a defined goal or a particular activity (the critical driver). A KPI is a numerical assessment over a period of time of some levels of operational goal.

We now cover the critical drivers and KPIs you should monitor for your efforts on LinkedIn.

Social-selling index

This is a feature that LinkedIn offers, and it covers six critical drivers:

1 Your personal brand
2 Finding the right people
3 Engaging with insights
4 Building relationships
5 Industry SSI rank
6 Network SSI rank

Your social-selling index will give you a score out of twenty-five (the KPI) for each driver. It will also benchmark you against other industry peers and against your network overall. To access this feature, ensure you are logged onto your LinkedIn profile and open this link: https://www.linkedin.com/sales/ssi.

Profile rank

This critical driver will show where you rank among your connections, although you should not be too concerned about reaching number one in this driver. The more pre-eminent your connections the more difficult it will be to rise in this ranking, but overall you should be seeing improvement in this area. The KPIs to monitor and score:

• Number of connections
• Your ranking among those connections
• Percentage ranking

Your number of connections should be improving every month, and your percentage ranking should be, too, even if your overall rank declines. A sensible goal is to be in the top one percent among your connections; this is more important than having a specific ranking number.

To view your profile rank, go to the Profile tab and in the dropdown menu select Who's Viewed Your Profile. You will then see the tab How You Rank for Profile Views.

Professionals like you

This will show where you rank among your industry peers in your country; obviously the higher your ranking the better. To access this driver go to your Profile tab, select Who's Viewed Your Profile and then Professionals Like You.

Profile strength

As we covered earlier, this indicator should show how well your profile has been completed. All Star is the only acceptable ranking, and if you've followed all of the steps I have outlined you should already be at this level.

Profile views

This is one of the most important metrics, and it affects almost all other drivers. Once we get into the daily tasks you'll see just how central this driver is to the success of this methodology. When we implement this methodology for our clients our goal is to exceed 2,000 views per 90 days. LinkedIn will track this driver for you, and show a weekly breakdown, plus a 90-days moving total. It's updated every day by dropping the number of views you had 90 days ago and adding the views from yesterday. It's a dynamic and ever-updating number.

To view this score, go to your Profile tab and in the dropdown menu select Who's Viewed Your Profile.

Keeping records

These are the six critical drivers and thirteen KPIs to monitor within LinkedIn. I suggest you go to these areas now and record your numbers in a spreadsheet you can keep adding to. To make this process as simple as possible, put your opening scores in the first column and update them on the first of every month going forward once you commence your daily tasks. List your categories on the left-hand side of your spreadsheet and enter your scores on the right. Your first entries should look something like this:

Social selling index	31/100
Your personal brand	12/25
Finding the right people	11/25
Engaging with insights	09/25
Building relationships	06/25
Industry SSI rank	Top 12%
Network SSI rank	Top 18%
Profile rank	121/236
Connections	127

Percentage ranking	Lower 47%
Professionals like you	30/99
Profile strength	All Star
Profile views	34

Now you need to create a second spreadsheet with the following fields across the top of the page:

Date connected	Date 2nd message	Daily contact list	Message sent	Date 3rd message	Message sent

We will cover this in more detail in the next chapter, but for now it's just another step in preparing for success. The three date columns are for inputting current and future dates. The daily contact list will be for links to your connections' profiles. You'll put an X in the message-sent columns when you've completed the daily task.

This spreadsheet doesn't need to be complex. Keeping it simple ensures that you're tracking the truly important information only and not irrelevant data just for the sake of tracking data. Unless the information you're tracking is of regular use, don't waste your valuable time on it.

Scripts

You're going to need five pre-scripted messages that you will be using on a daily basis. Having these preformatted will save you hours of work every week, and ensure you're consistent in your voice and messages. At the appropriate time, which we will outline in the daily tasks, you will simply copy and paste these messages as you interact with your new connections.

The point of these messages is to build trust, add value, and create connection and conversation with your new connections. None of these messages should in any way be a sales pitch for anything you sell.

The connection-request script

This will be the message you send to people you want to connect with. The majority of people use the very impersonal and almost insulting message that LinkedIn preformats for you. I'm sure you've seen it many times yourself when people have requested to connect with you. It goes something like this:

Hello Adam Houlahan

I'd like to add you to my professional network on LinkedIn.

Your acceptance rate from potential new connections will be infinitely higher if you send them a more personal and warm message that also outlines your reasons for wanting to connect. It doesn't need to be *War and Peace*; one or two sentences will be more than enough. The most important thing is to personalise each message with the new connection's first name only, and take away any fear that you're going to be pitching them with sales offers. Here's an example of one I use:

Hi Paul

I came across your profile recently and thought there might be some value in us being connected here on LinkedIn. I only share free and up-to-date content on social media for business.

Sincerely
Adam

Okay, now it's your turn to create your connection-request script ready for the next steps. Store it on your computer where you can access it easily each day. I suggest right on your desktop to save time searching through files everyday.

The welcome script

This message will be sent to all your new connections, regardless of whether you send a connection request and they accept, or you just accept a connection request. The majority of people miss the opportunity to start a conversation by simply thanking their new connections and going no further. Even worse, there are far too many people who have no concept of creating trust, value and conversation. These are the rookies who connect and then immediately send out their sales pitch, but hopefully this is not you. You would think that the almost-zero response rate this elicits would be the cue to change tack and try something more professional.

Your version should be warm, sincere and pitch free. There really is only one wrong way to do this, as we have just outlined. The only other mistake would be in failing to personalise the message with your new connection's first name only.

Here is an example of one message I use, which incorporates true pre-eminence and giving (the positive feedback I get from this message is always very heart-warming):

Hello Tanya

Thank you for connecting
When you did, something GREAT happened. You have helped prevent blindness in 10 children by providing them with a rich source of vitamin A. Not only have you stopped children from becoming visually challenged, but you've also increased their ability to fight infection, which will improve their chances of survival from a serious illness.
All of this (and more) has been made possible through my lifetime partnership with the Global Giving Initiative. B1G1: Business for Good (www.B1G1.com).
I believe that every business has the power to change lives by giving back through its everyday business

activities. Doing this together with you is a simple but powerful example of putting this belief into action. So again, thank you; not just for connecting here on LinkedIn, but for also making a huge difference in a child's life.

Together, we've made a huge impact.

Sincerely
Adam

Now create your own welcome-message script ready for the next steps. Add this to the document you just created for easy access.

Congratulations message

Every day LinkedIn will send you a reminder and give you links to anyone who is a first-degree connection who has a birthday or work anniversary. Sending the standard message that LinkedIn creates for you is, as with everything else, about as impersonal as it gets. I'm sure you've received your share of these messages, and I'm equally sure that you were unlikely to respond to or remember anyone who sent them.

Again, when you take the time to send someone a personalised message, you stand out from the crowd. More importantly, you receive responses from these people, even if it's simply to thank you for your kind thoughts. It doesn't need to be a long message; in fact, a short punchy version is preferable. Here is a message I often use:

> Hi Paul
>
> Congrats on your awesome milestone today. Wishing you every success today and for the rest of the year, too.
>
> Sincerely
> Adam

Now it's over to you. Create your version of a congratulations message before we move onto the next phase.

Free gift message

As you can see, none of these messages has anything to do with promoting products or services; they are all designed to create trust and conversation. The free-gift message, however, is designed to deepen the connection by offering a free gift of some description. It's also designed to move your connection and conversation away from LinkedIn and onto your database.

There is something everyone should always be aware of, whether we're talking about LinkedIn or any other social-media platform you use: we do not own our profiles on these platforms. If you took the time to read those deliberately long terms and conditions you must acknowledge before being given access to your account, you would see this for yourself.

The reality is that LinkedIn owns your LinkedIn profile, Facebook owns your Facebook account, and Twitter owns your Twitter accounts. The same is true of every other social-media profile you use. These companies can and do change the rules regularly, and your ignorance of these changes is rarely, if ever, a defence if you inadvertently break a rule you did not know existed. You can also find that what you're doing was okay last month but it's not okay this month.

The only thing you can truly own is your website and your database, so it makes sense to move as many of your followers as possible across to these forums. You also want them to be legitimately subscribed to your email database. The free-gift message is designed to do exactly that.

The best way to get people to willingly subscribe to your database, via your website, is to give them something relevant and valued for free. To keep your costs down, this should also be something you can deliver electronically via email or that can be accessed via the web.

The type of free gifts will vary depending on your industry, but in general courses, white papers, subscriptions or anything else that in the normal course of business could be charged for and are relevant to your connections should be okay. You may choose to create a product specifically for this purpose, but keep in mind that the higher the perceived value by your connections the higher the rate of opt-ins you will receive.

Of course this doesn't mean you should start giving away your core products or services. You might have something you were selling previously but discontinued, which could be freshened up to be relevant in today's marketplace.

Here is one of my free-gift messages, which has been very successful; you may even have seen it before:

Hi Paul

I was looking at your profile again after we connected a couple of days ago, and thought I might reach out to you. Specifically, Paul, I thought this could be of enormous value for you.
I recently created a FREE LinkedIn Optimisation Tutorial, and you can find more information about it here: www. bit.ly/FreeLinkedInCourse.
If having a truly enhanced presence on LinkedIn is of any value to you, I know you'll find this a very useful gift. After you've seen it for yourself, but only if you find it useful, please feel free to forward it to any of your connections if you want to offer them a small gift, too.

Sincerely
Adam

If you don't already have something like this, don't let it stop you getting started with your LinkedIn strategy. You can come back and add this step later. You will also be able to offer it to all of your existing connections at that point in the future. If you do have a product you can use, just script your message ready for the next phase. If you don't, you can brainstorm with your team about something you can use.

A keep-in-touch message

This last message is an easy one. It's very simple, and you should find it useful as a way of staying in touch with your ever-growing connections. With this message you'll give your connections a link to a great article of relevance once each month. Preferably it will be an article written by you that can be found on your website, but it could be any article on any blog or website as long as it's not on a competitor's site and contains information of value to your industry. You can even mix them up, choosing from your own content and other sites each month.

There should be nothing stopping you from getting started with this step. If you're not starting straightway with the free-gift message, this is where you can catch up once you do have something to offer.

Here is one of mine as an example:

Hi Jill

I recently wrote this article on social media for business and I received a larger than normal number of messages thanking me for the information. It occurred to me that you might also find this useful, so please do take a look to see if it has some relevance for you. I would value any feedback you have [insert link].

Sincerely
Adam

Each month you just update the link to a new article and change the message slightly. Take a look at your blog and find your best work to share. If you don't have a blog, find an industry-related article from a reputable source.

Once you have completed these messages, you're now ready to get started positioning yourself with pre-eminence and generating high-quality connections and new clients.

Chapter 8
GETTING STARTED

By now your profile should be looking very professional, and it will be optimised to add immense value for your current and upcoming connections. You have your scripts and offers ready, and good content is flowing regularly on your profile. You know your critical drivers and key performance indicators, and your spreadsheets are formatted. You're ready to start generating hundreds if not thousands of new leads, connections and then clients.

If you have followed all the steps to this point, you have probably invested more time on preparation before a marketing initiative than ever before. This preparation is critical to your success. If you skipped over any sections, thinking you would get back to them later, now is the time to review these and get them done.

If you're confident everything is in order, you're ready to get started. Let's begin.

Your client avatar

It should be obvious, but I'm still surprised at how often I have conversations with clients who cannot clearly articulate who their ideal clients are. So this is the process we follow to bed down this obvious yet crucial step.

Your client avatar will be a fictional representation of your best possible client. If you were in a room with a thousand business people, who were all there to network with each other, this is the process you would use to help you focus on connecting with the right people.

It's essentially a checklist; the more boxes you tick the more likely you are to be talking to the right people. It's possible to become highly specific in creating client avatars; however, this version is designed specifically to use within LinkedIn. Complete the following questions in relation to your ideal client.

What industries do they work in?

- Location
- Country
- City or town
- Position descriptions on LinkedIn
- Years of experience

Depending on what it is you do, and whom it is you work with, this list could be narrow or wide. For me it's a wide list, as I can and do work with multiple people in a number of countries and across a large number of industries. However, it is what it is for each person you deal with and each industry you operate within.

As an example, one of our clients is a restaurateur, so his clients vary widely by industry type, position description and years of experience. Their location is clearly defined, which is within a certain geographical distance of his business. No matter how great his food, clients are unlikely to travel from other countries, other states in Australia, or even beyond a certain distance from his location within his state.

By doing some research on his current client list, he was able to determine that the majority of his clients lived less than fifty kilometres from his restaurant, which made sense, so it would have been a waste of time for him to connect with people outside of this 50-kilometre radius.

Another client is in a particular niche of the medical profession, and he is not trying to connect with clients. Instead, he wants to connect with other doctors and medical practitioners as referral partners (in this case a better term than 'client'); he hopes they will refer their patients to him on occasion. In this client's field of medicine, people do travel long distances to consult with him because there are no surgeons with his specialised skills in every town or even city in Australia. Although he's looking for referral partners rather than clients, from the purposes of this exercise the same questions apply. The people he wants to connect with are very specific in terms of industry and years of experience; however, they cover a much wider range of locations than the restaurateur.

Now it's your turn to make a list of your ideal client, based on the above five questions. Once you have your answers, you're going to start finding them on LinkedIn.

The law of reciprocity

We covered this phenomenon earlier, but since it's an incredibly real and relevant part of this methodology it bears repeating. Unlike many marketing concepts that rely heavily on outbound techniques, what you're about to put into practice is the law of reciprocity in action. The law of reciprocity suggests that when you do something nice for someone, generally speaking they are highly inclined to return the favour, often in more generous ways than your original good deed.

Relative to what we're about to do on LinkedIn, this means that you will do much more than just push content and offers, or try to be everything to all people in the hope that some of them will be interested enough in what you do to take a look for themselves.

You now have a targeted list of the people who are highly likely to be the right type of client for you, and who will be interested in what you do—or at least you should have this list if you completed the last task we just set out. What you're about to do is now focus in on these people and do lots of nice things for them without trying to directly sell them your products and services.

Over time you will build their trust by supplying them with useful information, and acknowledging their skills, milestones and the value they bring to the table. So much so that they know who you are and what you do, they trust in your expertise, and many of them will request information about your services.

Others will refer you to their clients and friends, and supply that highly regarded third-party endorsement. Others still will become advocates and share your content with their connections, again as third-party proof of the value you bring. Yet more people will bypass the entire sales process, reach out and simply ask what are the next steps they need to take to work with you and your teams.

This is the law of reciprocity in its finest and almost mystical glory in action—working for you to create a consistent flow of your most sought-after clients, month after month, as long as you continue to follow the daily tasks we are about to cover.

There really is no magic overnight solution to creating leads and clients from LinkedIn. The process takes time to take effect, yet once the momentum builds it will create that consistent flow I just mentioned. Unfortunately many people who attempt to do this have very little success, but usually they fail because they take too short a view and revert to practices that turn most of their connections against them.

I have also seen programs that rely on spam-like practices that suggest it's okay to scrape email addresses from LinkedIn connections, and then start emailing them for a myriad of reasons. Regardless of what these people send their connections, this is a very unprofessional practice, and quite the opposite of everything this methodology does with great success. If their intention is to gain large numbers of email addresses for this purpose, they should be aware that more and more people, myself included, are starting to rebel and fight back by reporting people who abuse email contacts in this manner.

Daily tasks

We're now going to cover the simple step-by-step actions you need to do on a daily basis to make the magic happen. Whether you plan to do this yourself or have someone on your team do it, or even outsource to a virtual assistant, I strongly suggest you be at least partially familiar with the tasks. Do it yourself, at least for a short period of time. That way you'll be aware of the amount of time your teams should be investing and what the outcomes should be.

As soon as you commence these daily actions you'll start to see results relative to the critical drivers and KPIs we outlined earlier. The more consistent you are with these tasks the better your results will be. At the very least, you want to have this activity happening Monday to Friday. When we implement these strategies for our clients, we run most of the activities seven days per week, with the exception of major holidays.

Profile viewing

This is the fundamental driver of the law of reciprocity and so should always be one of the most important daily tasks you perform. Using the ideal client criteria you have just created, go to the Advanced Search tab on your profile. You will find it in the top right-hand side of your screen. Open this up and enter the search criteria. This might look something like:

Keyword: CEO
Location: Australia
Postcode: 4000
Second-degree connection

Choosing either second- or third-degree connection will ensure you're viewing profiles of people you're not already connected to. A search such as 'CEO' will generally deliver a very long list of profiles, but it will vary for every person based on second- and third-degree connections.

If I do this search right now, for all of Australia and third-degree connections, the resulting list shows 46,030 profiles. This would be a wonderful list to work through if these people were my ideal clients; however, regardless of the size of the list created LinkedIn will only allow users to view the first 1,000 profiles in that list. So in this instance I would miss out on the opportunity to connect with 45,030 of these people.

Limiting searches by postcode will display fewer results, but it still allows for viewing 1,000 profiles. If I now do the same search using this criteria, include only CEOs in Brisbane, and restricted that area to within fifteen kilometres of the city, my list reduces to 2,886 profiles. I could perform the same search using multiple other locations around Australia, effectively increasing my potential connections from 1,000 to a possible 30,000-plus.

Once you have your list, it's simply a matter of doing a right-click on the profile, selecting Open in a New Tab and working your way through as many profiles as you have time to view. When we do this service for our clients, our team aims to view 600 profiles per day, or around 4,000 per week.

When you do this, each person whose profile you have viewed will receive a notification that you have viewed their profile, with a link so they can view your profile in return. Most people don't get a lot of profile views, so some are bound to be intrigued enough to view your profile to see who you are. At this point, you will understand the need for your headshot and professional headline to be compelling since this is all they will see before clicking on your profile. The more professional your headshot is the higher the level of profile views.

When they do click on your profile, the next most important factor comes into play: your summary. If you have used the methodology I outlined earlier, you will be speaking to your potential connection in a language they understand. You will be outlining the problems they face regularly, and of course offering solutions to those problems. Many people will now read more of your profile, and some will send you connection requests, which is exactly the action you want.

Check your messages

Within a few days of following these daily tasks, you'll find you're getting a lot more messages each day than ever before, although some of these people will do exactly the opposite of what I consider good practice and immediately pitch you their products or services. Unless they're offering something of high value to you, just ignore these messages.

Others will reply politely to your messages, however, and you can use your own judgement as to when and whether you should respond.

Some messages will be requests for information or further correspondence with you, and these are the messages you need to action regularly. You will also find that with more and more messages coming in, these can easily get lost among other notifications you're receiving.

The best way to start the task of checking messages is to open the Message tab, then Unread Messages, and this will collate the messages without the clutter of other notifications, ensuring you don't miss any.

Another handy feature of LinkedIn is tagging, which allows you to create a list of profiles that you can find easily. You can have as many different tags as you like and there is no end to the ways you can use this feature. You could split them up under industry tags, or you could do what I do and use tags like 'Potential Client' and 'Client'. When someone has expressed interest in our services, by tagging them as a potential client I can easily find them on a regular basis and follow up with them as necessary. Tagging actual clients ensures I don't send these people irrelevant information in the future.

To create a tag list, go to your contacts page and hover over any profile in the list. On the left-hand side you will see the Tag tab. Click on this and it will give you the option of creating new tags; create all of the tags you intend to use. You can always add more at a later date, when you've become more proficient in using tags.

Once you have your tag list, you can add or remove someone from your tags at any time. Click on their profile and in the relationship section you will see the Tag tab. Use this to remove or replace the current tag with an updated version.

Accept connection requests

Your next task is to accept the new connections you will receive each day. In the top-right corner you'll find the tab you need to go to. It will have a number beside it, which is the number of connection requests you have. This icon is just to the left of your profile image icon, and looks like a silhouette of a person's head and shoulders. When you click on this tab you can choose to connect with all new connection requests, or you can simply read through these people's profiles to see if they're a good fit for you.

I personally connect with a large number of people who send me requests to connect with me on LinkedIn. If these connections turn out to be fake profiles or spammers, I simply unconnect from them. It's entirely up to you how you handle connection requests.

Connecting with potential clients

I have already covered the fact that some people will be intrigued enough to view your profile in response to you viewing theirs, and will send you a connection request; however, some will view your profile and not send you a connection request. The next step is for you to send *them* a connection request.

You will have your script ready for this, so go to your Who's Viewed Your Profile tab to see everyone who has viewed your profile. Scroll down to the views from yesterday and send a connection request to anybody on this list whom you feel is a good fit for you. Because they have viewed your profile just the day before, many will accept your request if you personalise your connection message.

Others will already be connections, and you'll be able to tell these from the '1st symbol' beside their name. They will also have a big blue clickable tab at the bottom of their profile image that says 'message'. Any profiles that show the word 'connect' are the ones you should focus on.

Congratulations message

There is value in doing these tasks in the order I am outlining them, and these next three steps will demonstrate the main reason for that. By doing the above tasks first you can do the following tasks in one step instead of three.

If you now navigate to your connections page via the My Network tab, the first thing you will see is a list of all the people in your network who have a birthday or work anniversary. You can now use your birthday or work-anniversary scripts to send personalised messages. Work your way through as many as you intend to send today. Once you've finished, stay in this section for the next task.

Welcome messages

Below all of your connections who have an anniversary will be your new connections. It should have defaulted to Sort By Recently Added. If for any reason it has not, select this option now.

All of your newest connections will now be in the order in which they became a new connection. You can now click on their profile and send them your scripted welcome message, personalised specifically for them. You'll want to ensure you do this all in one step, because it will continue to update throughout the day.

After the first day, you want to take note of the first person you sent your welcome message to, as this will be an easy way to ensure you welcome all of your newest connections tomorrow. And then tomorrow, start at the top of this list and send welcome messages until you reach the person you highlighted from the day before. In the beginning this may not be a large number of people, but as you continue the process this list will get longer each day. Currently I receive between twenty and thirty new connections per day.

Updating your spreadsheets

The final task to do in this section is add all of your new connections to your spreadsheet. The best way to do this is right-click on each profile and select Copy Link Location, paste this link into your spreadsheet, and when you send your next messages it will be as easy as clicking directly on the link from your spreadsheet.

Once you have all of these new connections in your spreadsheet, add today's date in the first column and copy to all new connections. Then choose the future dates to send your second and third messages and add them.

Free-gift messages

While you're still in your spreadsheet, you can go back to your previously added new connections that have today's date earmarked for your next message. This should be your free-gift message. Open up your scripted message and copy it, then open each person's profile from the link you have added to your spreadsheet and paste your message again, remembering to personalise it with their first name. Continue until you have sent your message to each person in your list.

Third message

You can now do the same with your third message by scrolling up your list until you come to the profiles with today's date. Of course, in the first week or two, depending on the timing of your second and third messages, these steps will not be necessary. Once you get to the first list of messages, however, this will become a daily task.

It's unlikely that you will want to do these tasks on your weekends, and it's quite okay to leave them until Monday, although it will mean you have more to do on Monday than any other day. To make this easier, it's a good idea to get into the habit of ensuring that when you future-date your new connections in your spreadsheet, you skip weekend dates on the two days of the week where this date would be a Saturday or Sunday, and make it the following Monday instead. If Monday is going to be a holiday, skip the date to Tuesday.

So that's it for your daily tasks. If you follow this process consistently, your profile views, connections and new-client list will grow before your eyes. With the exception of the profile-viewing task, everything else should take you less than thirty minutes per day, Monday to Friday.

Chapter 9
OUTSOURCING

Right about here is where people will say, 'Wow, LinkedIn is amazing, but it would take me hours every day to do all this.' Yes, it would, but depending on where you are in your business journey there are simple ways to solve this problem.

You could have an underutilised person on your team carry out these tasks for you each day. Or you could split the tasks between two or more people. We offer a service where we run this entire process on your behalf. If you would like further information, email us at clientdelight@ webtrafficthatworks.com.

The profile-viewing task is critically important, but it's something you could consider outsourcing to virtual assistants. Although it's a simple process, it's not a particularly good use of your time to do this for a few hours every day of the week. I know of a number of people who have given the profile-viewing tasks to their teenage children to do in return for weekly pocket money.

I do, however, suggest that you do your own profile-viewing to start with. It will give you a good sense of what constitutes optimal results, and you'll know the amount of time it should take your team, kids or VAs if you choose to use them.

Finding virtual assistants

Finding virtual assistants is very easy to do, and LinkedIn is the perfect place to source them. Just do an advanced search with the keyword phrase 'virtual assistant' and for the country select 'the Philippines'. You should have plenty of candidates to choose from, but take a good look at their profiles before sending them a connection request.

When you do send a request, in your message state that you're looking for some assistance with tasks on LinkedIn. I guarantee you will have near a one-hundred-percent acceptance rate. Make sure you ask for references from other clients they have worked for, and follow them up with an email or call. Reliability is the key value you want in your virtual assistant, and a word of warning: this can sometimes be an issue.

Once you have selected your assistant you need to give them very specific instructions. I find it's often best to start with just the profile-viewing task as a test, and if you're happy with their work you can consider adding some or all of the other tasks as well.

There are also companies that specialise in virtual-assistant services. Ezy VA is one, and there are others. They will look after all of the management for you so you waste almost no time in the daily process of monitoring LinkedIn. Understandably, the hourly rates will be higher if you hire a company to do this for you, but exactly how much will depend on the level of input you choose to have in the process.

If you're not already using a virtual assistant to handle many of the less critical tasks in your business, it's one of the best decisions you can make.

113

You'll find that many tasks can be outsourced at a fraction of your current hourly team rates, freeing up time for your best people to focus on more important income-generating activities. If you don't need full-time or even part-time additions to your team right now, using virtual assistants can be a great way to fill in the gaps until you're ready for a new team member.

Account security

One thing you should consider carefully whenever you contract anyone outside of your normal employ is the issue of handing over your LinkedIn password. When you do this, you're effectively handing over full control of very sensitive public profiles. It should go without saying that you need to ensure you're partnering with reputable virtual-assistant companies or individuals at all times.

I have heard of and been asked for assistance from many people who have fallen victim to unscrupulous use of their social-media profiles by the wrong people. I even know of people being held to ransom by companies and people they deemed trustworthy, where they have been prevented from having access to their social-media profile, websites and customer-relationship management systems.

There are, however, easy ways of keeping full control of your online assets. There are three tools I use and can recommend. I suggest you at least try the free versions of these tools to see if they have value for you and your organisation:

1 **LastPass** (www.lastpass.com) is a secure way to give anyone access to your login credentials without revealing any passwords. Any respectable virtual-assistant service will use and be open to using password-protection software like LastPass. There are three levels with this product: a free version, an annual-fee level, and an enterprise level. The software allows you to control the level of access any member of your team has to sensitive information. It's a very good security measure to use for almost anyone requiring login access to any online services you use.

2 **Teamviewer** (www.teamviewer.com) is also a great way to allow access to a computer or servers you can maintain control over. In some circumstances, allowing overseas or even inter-state access to some online programs, especially LinkedIn, can trigger security warnings or account lockdowns. By allowing access to your accounts via Teamviewer only, however, you are effectively limiting access to a geographic location of your choice.

If for any reason you need to remove someone's access to your system, you simply change the password and they no longer have that access. You can also control exactly when someone has access by turning Teamviewer off whenever you choose. There are also three levels of service with Teamviewer: free, paid for and enterprise.

3 **Hootsuite** (www.hootsuite.com) is another way you can share access to your social-media profile without giving password access. This very solid and robust program allows you to set up teams and give different levels of access to those who need it only.

A great advantage with Hootsuite is that you can load the content being shared on your social profile in advance, giving you time to vet content if required.

Hootsuite offers a free option, plus many different levels of paid services, including enterprise where required. You can also generate excellent reports customised to your specific needs.

Chapter 10
MOVING THE CONVERSATION OFFLINE

O nce you've begun implementing your *LinkedIn Playbook* strategy you will have a lot more conversations with your new LinkedIn connections. While LinkedIn does have its own customer-relations management platform of sorts, it's far better to start moving these conversations beyond the LinkedIn platform.

As we covered earlier, you do not own your LinkedIn profile or any other online platform other than your website and your database, which means keeping all of your connections, conversations and databases on LinkedIn, or any other social-media platform for that matter, is a huge risk. The rules can and do change all the time, as does the functionality of the platforms. Something that's working quite nicely for you today may disappear tomorrow.

Email and phone, however, will always stand the test of time. With the permission (and I stress *with the permission*) of your connections, you should be transferring their details into your CRM systems and moving the conversations to email, Skype and your phone.

As we covered earlier, simply taking your connections' information and dumping it into a sales funnel will not position you with pre-eminence, or achieve many sales or referrals. Some of your connections will have taken up your offer of a free gift and willingly moved across to your database. Others who may not take up your offer, however, will interact with you sometimes on LinkedIn. When this occurs I suggest you take the opportunity to move the conversation offline.

There are two ways you can achieve this. When appropriate, ask your connection to send you more information via your email address. I usually do this by responding with some thing like: 'Thanks for your message, James, that does look interesting and I was wondering if we could continue this conversation via email.' I then provide my email address.

This is almost always a successful way of transferring the conversation to email, where I can continue the conversation and keep better and permanent records of these conversations. I check emails a lot more regularly than messages on LinkedIn, and it also makes it easier for me to include my team where necessary.

The second option is to do the reverse, and ask your connection for permission to send them something of value by email. I usually do this by responding with something like: 'Thanks for your message, James, that does look interesting and I appreciate you taking the time to send it to me. I was wondering if we could continue this conversation via email. I recently wrote a blog post that you might find useful. With your permission I would like to send you a link to this, and it would be coming from my email address.' I then add my email address.

Your next task is to create two or three standard replies that can be used by you or your team in the right circumstances. The easiest way to do this is simply to wait until an opportunity arises to send this type of reply and keep a record of it at that time. I assure you this will happen very soon once you've commenced your daily tasks.

Once you're happy with your replies, you could choose to trial a couple of different options and see which ones get the best response rates. Add those ones to your scripts so your team can help you going forward.

How and when to ask for the call

As you progress along this journey the time will come when you should move from LinkedIn or email correspondence to a face-to-face meeting. The most common scenario is to have a 'meeting' through Skype, Zoom or Facebook, which seems to be as close as we get these days to an actual in-person meeting.

Not surprisingly, many people are hesitant to accept such invitations. A Skype call is almost like a face-to-face meeting, and we've all become comfortable with the relative anonymity of the online world. Getting your connections to agree to these meetings requires the full implementation of the seven hours, or eleven touch points, defined as the 'zero moment of truth' (you'll recall Google's research in the earlier chapter).

By this point you will have supplied enough quality information and free gifts, and/or solved enough of your connections' immediate problems, to gain their trust and respect, increasing your chances of a connection agreeing to progress to the next step. Suggesting any form of face-to-face meeting prior to this will, in the majority of cases, result in a deafening silence.

On the other hand, pre-eminent leaders often have the opposite experience, where they are asked to have a face-to-face meeting without needing to create that level of trust and respect beforehand. Often this is due to trust and respect being beyond question for these people. While this is a lovely position to be in, as a pre-eminent leader in your field it's still your responsibility to ensure you respect your connections and are giving them the best service and experience possible.

If you are indeed a pre-eminent leader, when faced with requests for face-to-face meetings you could be tempted to move directly to the sales conversation. In my experience, moving ahead too quickly often leads to short-term relationships. Instead, take the time to ensure your connection has all of the information they need, and has developed real trust and respect in your position as the person most qualified to solve their problems. This will achieve two important things.

1 It will change the eventual sales conversation from the standard sales pitch, where you justify your service and price, to the pre-eminent sales conversation we covered earlier. Price is no longer a factor, and the process has already convinced your connection that you have what they need. In other words, you have their trust.

2 It will ensure your connection and soon-to-be client understands that your time is worth something, and that you value sharing some of it with them.

I have found that sticking to this process of providing enough value first almost always delivers long-term, high-quality clients. I recall a recent conversation during the process of writing this book. This person, whom I will call Ben, called at the exact time I was expecting a call from an existing client. Ben opened the conversation by telling me that he had read a lot about me and had just been on my website. He said his business was suffering and he needed some assistance. I listened politely until he came to the point. Finally he said, 'So tell me, Adam, in sixty seconds convince me you're the man for the job.'

Ben was desperate for a solution, yet he was still motivated to find that solution to his problem at the lowest possible cost. Had I entertained his question, I would have been competing on price and inviting him to shop around to see if he could get a better deal. For all I knew, I could have been the third or fourth person he had spoken too.

Ben never became a client, and I didn't waste any time, other than those few minutes on the phone, trying to convince him to become one. In fact, I suggested he did shop around. I ended the call by saying I would be happy to take some time to get to know what he needed and could provide him with some free resources he would likely find of value. I could then organise a discovery session with him, and let him know the cost and how to book that session online.

Many of our clients come via referrals from pre-eminent people and existing clients. Almost always this is the best way to start a relationship; however, it is still a good idea to step these people through a process of discovery and trust building. Investing your time and skills at the beginning means you understand their needs and how best you can provide world-class solutions. It also ensures that the value proposition has nothing to do with price.

The right time to ask for that sales conversation is always after you have interacted with the potential client for at least seven hours, or had eleven interactions. It should never happen before this point, regardless of whether the person has requested the call with you, or you are requesting the call from them.

The steps you are following in this *Playbook* are designed specifically to start you on the journey to the awesome sales conversation in the right way. Once you have moved the interaction offline, you will be well on your way towards having that conversation. Unfortunately, the majority of people trip at this final hurdle. The way you ask for that conversation will often make or break the final outcome. Here is a real-life example, taken from a recent experience.

I was contacted by an enterprise that provides a service for social-media companies like ours. It was a start-up business, but from the initial conversation I decided that their product seemed worthy of further investigation so I had one of our team find out everything they could about the business online. By the time this was done we had invested quite a few hours, and I was ready for and open to the sales conversation.

When their sales manager asked if I would be willing to speak directly with him, I said I would and asked what was the best way to do that. Given that they were in the United States and I was in Australia, a conversation required dealing with the difference in time zones. I deal with companies and people in the United States on a weekly basis, so I knew roughly the times that were going to work, which was early morning for me and mid to late afternoon for him. This is his actual email reply:

Thanks, Adam

I am really looking forward to explaining further the value of our software ... I know you are going to love it. I can do a call next Wednesday at 11am, or Thursday at 2pm, which time suits you best?

Sincerely, James

James had made no effort, despite knowing that I lived in Australia, to work out what time his eleven am or two pm would be for me. And because he had never shared exactly where in the US he was, I had to spend time over the next few days emailing back and forth simply to make an appointment.

If you find yourself dealing with international clients it's paramount that you make this process seamless and painless. Find out in advance the difference in time zones to minimise the need for excessive correspondence. It makes no difference if you only deal with clients in one country, or one town or city. The more correspondence you generate in arranging for a sales conversation, the more opportunities you generate to lose the deal.

Fortunately there is a simple solution that transcends the challenge of country, time zone, and multiple emails. It's called 'meeting scheduling software' and there is no shortage of options. Just do an online search for exactly this term and take your pick. They range from simple and free to extremely integrated solutions for websites and other platforms.

I use Schedule Once (www.scheduleonce.com). It's easy to set up, and I receive many comments from clients praising the simplicity and ease of booking times that suit us both. Schedule Once will also send reminders to your client leading up to your agreed times, and allow a one-click addition to their chosen calendar. Should either of you need to reschedule, this is simple and professionally handled, although I suggest that only under extremely important circumstances should you ever reschedule a sales-conversation call.

Skype versus phone

When it comes time to have that all-important sales conversation, the options come down to phone, Skype or other forms of online communication. I find Skype to be universally preferred over most other forms of communication. Facebook is probably the second option, but generally most business owners prefer Skype.

It really comes down to whether you should use the good old telephone or Skype. There are two important reasons why you should opt for Skype wherever possible and the phone as a last resort.

1 **It's easier.** Most of us find it less daunting to say no in a phone call than during a face-to-face Skype call. We're so used to annoying phone calls that we're more likely to say no than yes when using

the phone. In Australia, annoying phone sales calls have become so prevalent that we now have a free do-not-call register that anyone can sign up for. It's an offence for phone-sales operators to call any numbers on this register.

2 **No online access.** When you talk on the phone you don't have the option of sending your client links to online resources or documents during the call, and there are very good reasons why you would want the opportunity to do that.

Using Skype will not eliminate all rejections of your offer, but I assure you it will lower the rejection rate. Using Skype allows for more personal one-on-one conversations, and this in turn allows you to build rapport and read the mood of your client, what they are being receptive to in your presentation, and what is not resonating with them. Over time, as your presentation skills improve, you will increase your close rates by becoming more adept at reading the flow of your conversations (although that's a topic for a whole other book).

When you're face-to-face on a live Skype call you will also have your client's undivided attention, and it will be almost rude of them not to focus solely on you. Think of how many times you've multi-tasked while you're on a phone call and not been fully engaged in the conversation.

Depending on your presentation, or the flow of the conversation, it's useful to be able to refer to a website or online resource. Using Skype allows you to easily send a link or even a document directly to your client in real time, without losing their attention or having to jump to another screen and send emails.

The single most important value Skype affords, however, is getting the paperwork completed after your new client says yes. How many times can you recall completing a successful sales conversation, advised you would send over your service agreement, contract, invoice or whatever was your next step, only to have nothing further occur? Buyer's remorse, other priorities, or the client simply changing their mind can and does occur.

I've always found that taking those few extra minutes to get pen to paper in the digital sense, while the client is in an agreeable mood, results in far fewer lost opportunities, delayed payments or new rounds of endless follow-up emails that waste valuable time.

If possible, you should offer your client the option of signing up to receive your product or service directly on your website. This gives you the opportunity to send them a direct link and walk them through every section live, and get the signature while still on your call. If you absolutely must have a written agreement then get with the times and use digital-signature software programs. There are many different versions of this type of software, but not all are user friendly. Before you commit, make sure the software is simple for your client to use. I recommend DocuSign (www.docusign.com), which is very user friendly and supported in many countries.

If you have not closed a sale online before, I highly recommend having a few practice runs with friends or family. Make sure you include transferring files and a walk-through of how your client will need to interact with your chosen digital program. You should also record your practice conversations and watch them on completion. Pay particular attention to your body language throughout, especially when you ask for the deal. Confidence will win you deals, but during a live presentation with a potential new client is not the best place to practice.

Seven steps to a pre-eminent sales conversation

Now you have all of the tools you need to position yourself with extreme credibility. You have a powerful lead-generation machine at your disposal, scripts for every step of the process, and the tools to create an exceptional sales funnel right up to the all-important sales conversation. You have everything you need to get to the Holy Grail, or the money step, as I like to call it. All you need to do now is have that conversation.

A simple reality is that not a great deal of high-value business is done in the online world; at some point it requires real, human interaction. The online world can and is a wonderful lead-generation and sales-funnel medium; however, the close requires tried and tested sales skills and that all-important face-to-face meeting, in whatever form it takes place.

There are sales conversations and there are pre-eminent sales conversations. You've done a lot of hard work to get to this point, so you might as well do what all pre-eminent people do and have an awesome sales conversation. So what is the difference between the two?

First you need to understand the two conversations that are happening at the same time, and why only one of them is where the successful outcome resides. The first conversation is obviously the one you are having with your potential new client. The second, and perhaps most important conversation, is the one your client is having in their head while they are talking with you.

Interestingly, this second conversation is often very much at odds with the first. In their head, your client will be addressing the negatives—all of the potential reasons for not wanting to work with you. To have an awesome sales conversation, you need to bring these issues into your actual conversation and make it a two-way dialogue instead of leaving the thoughts festering in your client's head.

Everything you've done to this point has been about building trust and credibility, and this is exactly what an awesome sales conversation focuses on. You already have the client's trust, and they already see you as a credible and reliable solver of their problem. So your pre-eminent sales conversation will not seek to pressure the client into making a hasty decision they may later regret. Instead, you will do as much listening as talking.

Here are the seven steps to follow when you create your conversations:

1 Acknowledge that your client's time is valuable, and reiterate that you have had a number of interactions prior to this meeting.

2 Outline what you understand to be the client's problem and ask if you have this correct. If not, ask them to give you more details so you can fully understand their needs.

3 Based on their answer to question two, before moving on ask for their confirmation that you now have a full understanding of the problems they currently need solved, and where they are positioned right now.

4 Outline how things are going to be once these problems have been resolved. In other words, create their new future reality that they can visualise and start believing in. Ask your client how it will improve their business once this situation is in place.

5 Ask more questions to bring out in the open any concerns or doubts your client still has.

6 Share a story of another client without breaking any confidentiality. Describe how the other person started out in a similar position, and explain how you were able to add massive value when you solved their problems. Outline that previous client's new reality as it now stands, and how you can see this being the same for your new client. Ask if this is the outcome they're looking for and how they would feel if you helped create this for them.

7 Ask for the sale.

It's as simple and elegant as that. If you have connected through Skype, you can now send through your service agreement, or your link to an online sign-up page on your website. Walk your new client through your sign-up process on the spot and welcome them into your fold.

I have used this simple formula myself on many occasions with great success, as have many of our clients. It's worth having a few practice runs through the seven steps to a pre-eminent sales conversation with friends or family before unleashing your newfound knowledge on your leads. A little preparation before your call will also help make a smooth transition from the sales conversation to the sign-up process.

While this step will vary for almost every business, the fundamental requirement is to get some form of agreement in place while you're still on the call, or at the very least to have it in the client's grasp in a format that's simple to complete and return electronically. You or members of your team can follow up with the rest in due course.

The elegant gift

I added this final step to my sales process soon after joining B1G1. On almost every occasion, it has been been greeted with such gratitude, tears and joy that I couldn't imagine ever removing it from our company now. It is the gratitude certificate. I simply choose a giving program hosted by B1G1 that has some degree of alignment with either our new client's business or the product they have entrusted me to deliver. As an example, here is the message we sent to a client who is a doctor:

I am really honoured to be working with you to build an exceptional online brand presence. While this is what I do, I want to let you know why I do it. It's the why that underpins everything.

[Client's name], I believe real and meaningful change comes through the world's entrepreneurs; people just like you. My purpose is to help them create a powerful online presence that grows and accelerates their global footprint so that together we really can make a huge impact.

To honour both you and that underlying why, I have provided 7,500 children with essential vitamins to assist blindness prevention. This gratitude certificate comes with sincere thanks as a record of our commitment.

This is, I believe, the final act of true pre-eminence and it will certainly position you as such. When a thoughtful gift is given to honour a new relationship after the fact, you create clients who become your greatest advocates. The law of reciprocity kicks into action once again, and your new client develops a burning desire to shout your praises to as many of their friends, colleagues and clients as possible, at every opportunity.

As we have already covered, referrals are possibly the most sought-after way to commence a sales conversation. Any form of third-party endorsement such as these cannot be bought, which means they have immense value.

I don't do it for these reasons, however; referrals are just a by-product of the act of giving in the most meaningful way. I never set out with the intention of generating referrals, and I would still do it if this never occurred. But the simple reality is that it does, and it will deepen in the most elegant way your relationships with your new clients before they have even begun.

PART II

The LinkedIn2Success Program

So there you have it. You now have all of the tools to create your very own LinkedIn playbook and commence marketing your products, services or yourself with pre-eminence. I have shared with you my best processes, and the methodology we use with our clients all over the world.

Many businesses want this as a done-for-you service; it's one of the products we offer and I'm happy to offer it to you, too. You may also know of business leaders or companies that require such a service, and you're very welcome to share this with them.

Web Traffic That Works is, you'll find, very different, and here is how our LinkedIn2Success program works.

First, we have a real purpose: to help you create a powerful online presence that grows and accelerates your global footprint so that together we can make a huge impact.

Second, we extend that impact by making sure that everything we do gives back in quite surprising ways, thanks to our lifetime partnership with Buy1GIVE1. In terms of how we do what we do, we understand that our clients have three key challenges:

1 They struggle to get high-quality leads at an affordable cost.
2 They don't have the time to add social-media marketing to their daily tasks.

3 They know that it takes time to create a highly professional presence online, but they want immediate results.

To solve these frustrations we designed our flagship program, Linkedin2Success, which creates solutions:

• Targeted new leads every day
• Professional online presence that the client's team can implement, or which we will implement for them
• Return-on-investment that ensures our services are an asset and not an expense

The program is an intensive 'deep dive'—a superb, results-producing methodology that creates a cutting-edge, lead-generation sales funnel for almost any industry. Of course, there is no cookie-cutter program that suits every business, and we know that yours is as individual as you are.

Sound interesting? Then claim your free discovery session and book an obligation-free Skype or phone chat so that we can listen, explore ideas, and customise things specifically for you. We think you'll be genuinely surprised by what you discover.

You will find further details in the members area on our website.

Case Studies

The following companies have all followed *The LinkedIn Playbook* methodology and have kindly shared with us their results. As you will see, they vary to a great degree in the products and services they provide, which is testament to the power of the process. It transcends many industries and countries, which should give you comfort in implementing your own version of the same.

Karl Schwantes

Xennox Diamonds

Karl Schwantes is a national award-winning designer with an uncanny eye for quality and uniqueness. His craft lies not just in making unique jewellery but also in connecting with people and taking them on a journey to find or create a special piece that tells a story. Over the last twenty-one years, he has helped over 5,700 couples find their perfect dream ring. From diamonds to creation and crafting, Karl is the ultimate guide when it comes to helping men create that perfect piece that their partners will love forever.

These were Karl's key performance indicators when he commenced the LinkedIn2Success program:

Social Selling Index	80/100
Your personal brand	22.23
Finding the right people	16.54
Engaging with insights	16.34
Building relationships	25
Industry SSI rank	Top1%
Network SSI rank	Top 3%
Profile rank	121 out of 1,484
Number of connections	1,484
Percentage ranking	Top 9%
Professionals like you	27
Profile strength	Expert
Profile views	209

These were Karl's key performance indicators after ninety days on the LinkedIn2Success program:

Social Selling Index	90/100
Your personal brand	24.08
Finding the right people	21
Engaging with insights	20
Building relationships	25
Industry SSI rank	Top 1%

Network SSI rank	Top 1%
Profile rank	24 out of 2,322
Number of connections	2,322
Profile percentage ranking	Top 1%
Professionals like you	Number 1
Profile strength	All Star
Profile views	1,584

After signing up to the Linkedin2Success program, I was easily able to upgrade my profile status to All Star. With Adam's guidance and the comprehensive resources guide, I noticed an immediate jump in my profile ranking. With this came a significant increase in LinkedIn engagement and requests for my custom design work. My new connections were also more interested in a number of my other skills, such as keynote speaking and bespoke experience packages. As I am often featured in the media, having a professional LinkedIn profile is essential. Media will often look at my profile prior to connecting for an appearance. This has been a central pillar in our marketing in moving from traditional print to our new PR strategy. Collaborative partnerships have also been an amazing by-product of working with Adam and the LinkedIn2Success program. I now get approached on a regular basis to work with leading brands in mutually beneficial promotions, whereas previously I was the one generating the interest.

I can wholehearted recommend Adam and the LinkedIn2success program. I have met many professionals in the LinkedIn space, but never before someone who has helped me in achieving such amazing results in such a short period of time. It is so refreshing to see someone who aims to offer the same level of service and dedication to surpassing their client's expectations as we do. I guarantee you won't be disappointed.

Callum Laing

Unity Group

Unity Group is a private-equity enterprise that focuses on helping small to medium businesses unlock the value of their businesses through mergers, acquisitions and agglomeration IPOs.

These were Callum's key performance indicators when he commenced the LinkedIn2Success program:

Social Selling Index	83/100
Your personal brand	11.8
Finding the right people	13.10
Engaging with insights	09.07
Building relationships	10.18
Industry SSI rank	Top1%
Network SSI rank	Top 3%
Profile rank	69 out of 4,571
Number of connections	4,571
Percentage ranking	Top 2%
Professionals like you	6th
Profile strength	Advanced
Profile views	1315

These were Callum's key performance indicators after ninety days on the LinkedIn2Success program:

Social Selling Index	86/100
Your personal brand	21.83
Finding the right people	21.00
Engaging with insights	18.00
Building relationships	25
Industry SSI rank	Top 1%
Network SSI rank	Top 2%
Profile rank	63 out of 6,995
Number of connections	6,995
Profile percentage ranking	Top 1%
Professionals like you	Number 1
Profile strength	All Star
Profile views	2,865

I had been on LinkedIn from pretty early on, but it was only in the last year that I started to use it more as a lead-generation tool. I had already put some work into my profile before working with Adam, but together we were able to significantly increase the volume of leads coming through. While the platform, like any other, is dynamic and we have had to tweak our approach several times, it is consistently generating quality leads.

One of the biggest advantages it offers is that when we reach out to our target market, it is very easy for them to quickly assess whether I am someone they would want to connect with. Since our targeting is very specific and I have built my profile to showcase the elements that would appeal, we have a very high conversion of people willing to connect and then meet in person.

I don't have the time to stay focused on the ever-changing social-media landscape, so working with a professional like Adam, who is constantly tweaking the system and trying things for me, allows me to stay ahead of the game.

Sue Sparrow

The Sparrow Group

The Sparrow Group is a national company that is innovative, modern, effective and flexible, which works with their clients on a one-on-one basis to ensure they have exceptional insurance that suits their specific requirements, providing an outstanding personal service. Not only do they specialise in the beauty and cosmetic-injecting nurses' industry, they also have general business insurance with a broad range of industry policies.

These were Sue's key performance indicators when she commenced the LinkedIn2Success program:

Social Selling Index	32/100
Your personal brand	08.02
Finding the right people	12.10
Engaging with insights	07.03
Building relationships	4.90
Industry SSI rank	Top1%
Network SSI rank	Top 3%

Profile rank	121 out of 182
Number of connections	182
Profile percentage ranking	Lower 40%
Professionals like you	No ranking
Profile strength	Intermediate
Profile views	18

These were Sue's key performance indicators after ninety days on the LinkedIn2Success program:

Social Selling Index	**80/100**
Your personal brand	18.42
Finding the right people	21
Engaging with insights	15.12
Building relationships	25
Industry SSI rank	Top 1%
Network SSI rank	Top 2%
Profile rank	17 out of 2,100
Number of connections	2,100
Profile Percentage ranking	Top 1%
Professionals like you	Number 1
Profile Strength	All Star
Profile Views	1,064

Firstly I would like to thank Adam and his team for putting up with my lack of understanding of how the program worked and assisting me with the utmost patience, not only through out the set-up time but also through the program.

I have found the LinkedIn2Success program amazing; Adam and his fantastic team worked their magic behind the scenes to ensure that I was profiled in a professional manner. Adam worked through the program step by step with me, with each 'next steps' also providing reminders if I got behind with the program.

My results have been outstanding. I am now building a very strong relationship with a new national company, which found me through LinkedIn where our synergies connect; the reflection of this relationship is a large number of new clients, with a number of strong referrals.

Due to our niche market, it can be challenging to break into new arenas; again, through the LinkedIn2Success program. The creditability that is building has been proved time and time again, by bringing in new clients constantly.

I believe our business contacts have doubled since commencing the program. I would encourage anyone that is serious about building their business to jump in with LinkedIn2success. You and your business will never be the same again.

Tim Gray

Prophit Systems Pty Ltd

Prophit Systems is a leader in supply-chain management (SCM) software. Their unique solutions simplify supply-chain processes and enable clients to manage issues and optimise opportunities.

These were Tim's key performance indicators when he commenced the LinkedIn2Success program:

Social Selling Index	46/100
Your personal brand	21.31
Finding the right people	11.93
Engaging with insights	03.41
Building relationships	09.48
Industry SSI rank	Top 21%
Network SSI rank	Top 21%
Profile rank	61 out of 378
Number of connections	378
Profile percentage ranking	Top 17%
Professionals like you	17th
Profile Strength	All Star
Profile Views	70

These were Tim's key performance indicators after ninety days on the LinkedIn2Success program:

Social Selling Index	81/100
Your personal brand	22.74
Finding the right people	21.00
Engaging with insights	14.72
Building relationships	22.4
Industry SSI rank	Top 1%

Network SSI rank	Top 3%
Profile rank	16 out of 1,267
Number of connections	1,267
Profile percentage ranking	Top 2%
Professionals like you	Number 1 in Australia
Profile strength	All Star
Profile views	1,605

Since adopting the Linkedin2Success program I have experienced a dramatic increase in referral leads. I have had a four-fold increase in the leads of potential partners, with many connections directly enquiring about their suitability to distribute my products.

Beyond the obvious and exciting increases in the channels to my business, I have found Adam to be excellent to deal with. He has been available when I've wanted his direction, and his advice has been both considered and highly valuable. Adam has redefined what I now expect from social-media support.

Beth Maclean

Timeless Legal Network

Our products are designed to help inspiring lawyers get back to why they went to law school: to earn a great living, make a difference and live a great life.

These were Beth's key performance indicators when he commenced the LinkedIn2Success program:

Social Selling Index	26/100
Your personal brand	07.71
Finding the right people	08.93
Engaging with insights	04.71
Building relationships	06.78
Industry SSI rank	Low 41%
Network SSI rank	Low 34%
Profile rank	98 out of 224
Number of connections	224
Percentage ranking	Low 43%
Professionals like you	No ranking
Profile strength	Expert
Profile views	38

These were Beth's key performance indicators after ninety days on the LinkedIn2Success program:

Social Selling Index	82/100
Your personal brand	21.33
Finding the right people	21.00
Engaging with insights	15.75
Building relationships	24.22
Industry SSI rank	Top 1%

Network SSI rank	Top 2%
Profile rank	7 out of 1,103
Number of connections	1,103
Profile percentage ranking	Top 1%
Professionals like you	Number 1 in Australia
Profile strength	All Star
Profile views	3,102

I came to social media late in the game, and with a healthy dose of scepticism. Before setting up my own firm, Timeless Legal Network, I worked as a lawyer for a top-tier law firm in Sydney. As the main rainmaker, I had managed to build up to over twenty people in a relatively short period of time. I had a good network and had maintained those connections over the years, so I was sure that with my own firm I would be ahead of the game. I was in for a surprise.

Before launching my business, I finished my website and started putting out feelers to my network. I also travelled to North America to speak to thought leaders in the profession and seek their support. It all went well until one of my supporters introduced me to a prominent businesswoman with a large number of lawyers on her customer list. We met via Skype and hit it off right away. She was intelligent and engaging, and she generously offered to help me in terms of supporting my new business. We talked about what we could do together.

Suddenly she said, 'Beth, I've just gone online and realised that you don't have a good social-media presence. Before I can introduce you to the people we've been talking about, you really need to develop that presence.

They'll expect that. Once you have that sorted, let me know and I'll introduce you then.'

I had not seen that coming. I had believed that my website, hard work and personal approach to business would be enough. It was not. I learned the hard way that by not having a good social-media presence I was missing out on important opportunities. Adam, and his Linkedin2Success Program, quickly gave me the social-media presence I needed. The program also created additional and sometimes unexpected opportunities for my business that I could not have achieved through standard marketing efforts.

I'm still learning the power of social media and the opportunities it can provide. As I said at the beginning, I came to social media with a healthy dose of scepticism. I am now a convert, thanks to Adam and his team.

Bonuses

Bonus 1

As I'm sure you are aware, all things social media move fast. What was relevant today may be old school six months from now. One of the challenges in writing about this fast-paced, dynamic and always improving juggernaut LinkedIn is exactly that—staying relevant.

To combat this challenge, and as part of your purchase of *The LinkedIn Playbook*, you have access to our playbook members area. You can access this at www.adamhoulahan.com.

This website is where we keep you up to date on all things LinkedIn, including case studies, best practice, and the changes that LinkedIn often make. Access is free for all who own a copy of *The LinkedIn Playbook*, so register today.

Bonus 2

If you would like to join the growing community that is www.B1G1.com and have access to the thousands of projects they support, Masami and the team have generously supplied an exclusive offer to owners of *The LinkedIn Playbook*. Go to www.B1G1.com and simply add the code word 'playbook' in the checkout section. You will see the lovely surprise waiting for you there.

My Gift to You

Thank you for purchasing a copy of *The LinkedIn Playbook*. I am truly honoured to share this journey with you. My first book, *Social Media Secret Sauce*, has been a wonderful success and I have received messages of gratitude from thousands of people around the world. It is very humbling to still be receiving such messages two years after its release. I do hope you find *The LinkedIn Playbook* equally useful, and please do share your thoughts with me now that you have read it.

You can always contact me through my website (www.adamhoulahan.com) or connect with me on any of my social profiles you will find on there, too.

Don't forget you have access to the new members' area on the website, simply use the code word 'playbook' to register for access. You will find more helpful resources there at your disposal and all the latest updates regarding LinkedIn as they are developed.

My first gift, which you will find in the members' area, is a link to download the free e-book *Social Media Secret Sauce*. Please enjoy it with my compliments.

And just by purchasing this book something great has happened: you have given eleven Cambodian girls a book for a day. The books depict Cambodian village scenes and stories culturally appropriate to the girls.

Some of the books have English translations that accompany them so that girls learning English can develop their skills further. The girls are extremely eager readers so there is a constant need for additional books. They love to share their developing language skills with their younger siblings as well as their parents and grandparents, who have never learned to read.

I believe real and meaningful change comes through the world's entrepreneurs, people just like you. My purpose is to provide your businesses with powerful tools to grow and accelerate your global footprint.

Through my lifetime partnership with the global giving initiative B1G1, I am well on track to positively impact the lives of more than one million people in need. Doing this with you is a simple yet powerful way of putting this belief into action. So I thank you, not just for purchasing the book but also for positively impacting these young girls' lives. Together we have made a huge impact.

As you may know, I love quotes. I share them daily and have a few favourites I live by, so until the next book here is one of my favourites I would love to share with you:

'Be yourself; everyone else is already taken.' —Oscar Wilde

About the Author

ADAM HOULAHAN is an international keynote speaker specialising in social media for business, and CEO of the highly successful agency Web Traffic That Works. He resides in Australia's famous tourist destination, the Gold Coast, Queensland, and is considered one of Australia's leading experts on harnessing the power of LinkedIn for business. Over three thousand people globally have sought his assistance to leverage the power of LinkedIn for their businesses.

Adam is also a featured columnist for *MOB Magazine*, an Australian business publication. He consults on social media to private clients in Australia, New Zealand, North America, the Middle East and Singapore. As CEO or owner of six successful companies, he has developed the hands-on experience to understand business from the inside.

Adam believes real and meaningful change will come through the world's entrepreneurs. His purpose is to provide their businesses with powerful tools to grow and accelerate their global footprint. And that together we make a huge impact.

Through his lifetime partnership with the global giving initiative B1G1, he intends to positively impact the lives of more than one million people in need.

Adam has been interviewed on numerous podcasts, radio shows and webinars, and has spoken at over one hundred events, including Malaysia Social Media Week, Podcast Revolution, Royal Caribbean International and for Dent (acknowledged as 'the world's leading personal brand accelerator' by *The Huffington Post*).

See many of these interviews at www.adamhoulahan.com/media. Connect with Adam at www.adamhoulahan.com/connect.

CPSIA information can be obtained
at www.ICGtesting.com
Printed in the USA
LVOW13s0429160817
544948LV00042B/929/P